People Becoming The Church

By Wes Davis

ISBN-10: 1978445156
ISBN-13: 978-1978445154

TABLE OF CONTENTS

ACKNOWLEDGEMENTS

AUTHOR'S NOTE

SECTION ONE | QUESTIONS

Question #1: Why don't people go to church? • 11

Question #2: How do people become the church? • 21

Question #3: What difference does a church make anyway? • 33

SECTION TWO | 12 CHALLENGES

Challenge #1: Say yes everyday—Follow Jesus wherever he leads • 55

Challenge #2: Teammate—Nobody does the mission alone • 71

Challenge #3: Good Neighbor—Meet real needs in practical ways • 87

Challenge #4: Gospel—Share good news with others • 101

Challenge #5: Generosity—Live a generous life • 119

Challenge #6: Mercy—Commit to forgiveness in all your relationships • 133

Challenge #7: Apprentice—Bring someone with you • 149

Challenge #8: Freedom—Choose to be free • 163

Challenge #9: Take Back Mondays—Reclaim the joy of work • 179

Challenge #10: Family—Love the family you have • 197

Challenge #11: Sabbath—Rest one day so you can enjoy the other six • 217

Challenge #12: Crazy Idea—Do what God made you to do • 239

SECTION THREE | STORIES

Share your stories + the People Becoming The Church Prayer • 253

ACKNOWLEDGEMENTS

Thank you to my wife, Kari—I love you with all my heart. You are and have always been by my side. Always. You make me want to be a better man. Let's grow old together.

Thank you to my children, Kalissa, Austin, and Klara. You are my greatest earthly treasure. Thank you for giving me the privilege to be your Dad and still have flaws. Thank you for letting me tell stories about our family that involve you. Yes—I will continue my deal to give you $1 for every time that I talk about you in one of my stories. And it appears that I already owe you each $1.

Thank you to my family. Mom and Dad—you sacrificed so much to give us every opportunity to succeed. Your life of unconditional love and faith in God has been the loudest voice in my life. To my sisters—we have so many stories. I love it when we sit around the table and say, "Remember when . . . ."

Thank you to the newlife family. Our love is real and our relationships are rich. You gave my family a grace-filled environment to thrive. It is an honor to be on the mission with Jesus together.

Thank you to my closest friends. You remind me that nobody does the mission alone.

Thank you Jesus.

You are my Lord, my Savior, and my King.

AUTHOR'S NOTE

Rick Warren, well-known pastor and best-selling author, once said to me, "If you write a book, don't try to write it for everyone, write it for your church. That way it will be personal. If it helps other people, that's up to God. But write the book to encourage your church – that's what God has called you to do."

It was more than a decade ago, but I never forgot that. It was a powerful moment for me. Powerful for me . . . and perhaps for everyone else in the room.

You see, Rick didn't even know he was speaking to me. I was one of a few thousand people in the room at Saddleback Church that day. But that's how I took it—a conversation—just the three of us. Rick. Me. And Jesus.

God spoke through Rick to me about this book. The only reason I didn't write it earlier is that I didn't know what to say. Actually, I knew what I wanted to say. I just hadn't lived enough of it yet.

Talk is cheap. But there is something about living it out that makes our words more powerful. More powerful and more expensive. Real love costs a lot.

It's just like God to do that . . .

Instead of saying I love you, he sent Jesus. (I would say that message stuck.) And it is even more powerful when you become part of it. It's "God so loved the world" but through you and me. And through everyone else who dares to follow Jesus. That is who this book is for.

This book is for all of the people becoming the church.

It's for you.

I think God wants to say something through your life.
Something
so powerful it will change you and everyone else who
dares to listen.

Because someday this world is going to need you at your full
potential. This book was written to help you get there.

SECTION ONE
QUESTIONS

After three days they found him (JESUS) in the temple, sitting among the teachers, listening to them and asking them questions.

LUKE 2:46 NLT

He who asks a question remains a fool for five minutes. He who does not ask remains a fool forever.

CHINESE PROVERB

INTRO - QUESTIONS

Do you like to ask questions or give answers? I think most people like to give answers. At least I do. I'm not exactly sure why. It probably has to do with wanting to feel smart and powerful, like I've got this. But the truth is I don't. And neither do you. None of us do. And that's okay. It's just not okay if we won't admit it. Because if we don't admit it, life will humble us.

Maybe that is why it's so crushing when something terrible happens and we get stuck on why.
Why did this happen?
    Where is God?
        Does he care?
            Or better yet, does God even exist?

These are really heavy questions, especially if we aren't used to picking them up. They can feel overwhelming and exhausting. But perhaps, these are really important questions we need to ask more often.

You know who asks lots of questions? Kids.

I still remember driving in the car with my oldest daughter (who was in the fifth grade at the time) and from the backseat of the car she asked me where babies come from. I felt totally unprepared for that moment, but at least I knew the answer. It was a big moment. And I had decided to be completely honest and level with her. I wanted her to hear it from her Dad. Did my answer surprise her? No. It horrified her. I can still hear her voice and corrective tone. "Uh . . . Dad, that's not what I was asking. And . . . that was way too much information."

Questions force us to stop and listen. The better the question, the longer the pause. The biggest questions always lead to more questions because they spark curiosity. Without curiosity, there is very little learning regardless of the answers.

Sadly, we were born with curiosity but at some point curiosity fades. We lose interest in being curious.

We stop asking questions like:
Why are we here?
How can I know if God is real?
What's next, after death?
What does it really mean to love someone?

Without curiosity, there are no questions.

You know who else asked a lot of questions? Jesus.
Reading one of the four gospels about Jesus is like reading one question after another.

Jesus asked a lot of questions.
And a lot of people asked Jesus questions. One hundred and fifteen questions to be exact.

Jesus was asked 115 questions in the Gospels and of those he answered 113.

There were only two questions he refused to answer:
"Are you the King of the Jews?" (Pilate—Luke 23:3, NLT)
"By whose authority do you do these things?"
(Religious leaders—Mark 11:28, NLT)

Why didn't he answer them?
I know. I'm curious, too.

Of the 113 questions Jesus answered, 52 of those questions he asked himself.

Does that crack you up? Almost half of the questions that Jesus was asked he asked himself. (Maybe that is what you have to do when people stop asking questions.)

Oh . . . and one other thing that Jesus did is this: when someone asked Jesus a question, he usually asked a question back. (Like he was playing Jeopardy).

Actually . . . that was the rabbinical style of teaching. Answering questions with questions causes students to dive deeper into learning. It's what Jesus does. Jesus rewards curiosity and honors disinterest.

Our questions reveal our hearts.

One question Jesus was asked was, "How does a person inherit eternal life?" It was a great question. It just wasn't a real question. (Luke 10:15, NLT)

Why? The person who asked the question was an expert in the law who had more answers than questions and only asked it to trap Jesus.

What did Jesus do? He didn't answer his question—at least not right away. Instead, he asked a question back, "How do you read it?"

The expert knew the answer. It was an easy one. A softball lob.

Love God and love your neighbor. And he was right. Jesus even told him he was right. But the expert wanted more than being right. He wanted Jesus to be wrong.

So he asked, *"Who is my neighbor?"* (Luke 10:29, NLT)

Our questions
reveal our hearts.

How did Jesus answer that? With a story.

Jesus told a story about a man who gets beaten, robbed, and left for dead. Two men, a lot like the expert (very religious), come by and see the beaten man, but they don't help. They simply walk by.

The only person who helps is someone the expert would despise—a Samaritan. This is someone who is racially, culturally, and religiously different. Not only are Jews and Samaritans different, they have a long history of despising one another because they were once part of the same Jewish nation that split.

The Samaritan might be your ex-spouse, your former employer, the friend who you think betrayed you, the person you are prejudiced against, or the person you struggle to forgive. I don't know who your Samaritan is, but I do know you definitely would not call them good.

That is the person, Jesus says, who saves your life.

And then Jesus answers the expert's question with a question.
"Who is my neighbor?" becomes
"Who was a neighbor to this broken man?"

The expert's reluctant answer: the one who showed mercy. It becomes a challenge to love. Jesus says, *"Go and do the same."(Luke 10:37, NLT)*

Really big questions do this. They challenge us to love. They make us uncomfortable. Questions like this force us to face our fears and our doubts. We have to grow, stretch, develop, change, and transform into something better.

Some people think that faith means never having

any doubts.

I used to think that, too. But strong faith doesn't come from unasked questions. Questions tell us it's okay to have doubts. Doubts don't make us weaker; they make us stronger.

I like what Tim Keller said about faith and doubt:

A faith without some doubts is like a human body without any antibodies in it. TIM KELLER (DOUBT: A SECOND LOOK AT DOUBT)

It takes courage to doubt. And it takes courage to ask hard questions.

Only the most courageous will ask the questions of the soul. These questions are so big you have to go somewhere even bigger to get answers. The biggest place I can think of is the ocean.

My wife, Kari, surprised me with a quick Oregon Coast getaway. Apparently she thought we might need a little romance (or as I put it—a little "additional" romance) in our marriage. So . . . she whisked me away to Lincoln City, Ore.

What an amazing place. We stayed right on the water in a hotel hanging over the cliffs . . . you could walk down stairs and boom! There's the ocean.

I still remember standing in front of that ocean . . .
  The sound of waves crashing.
    The smell of salt.
      The wind on my face.
        Ocean as far as the eye can see.

I like taking big questions to the ocean, because at the ocean

I don't have to try to feel big.

Everyone is small at the ocean. You can't get a big head when you're looking at the ocean. It's too vast. And at the ocean, you get different questions—even bigger questions. Nobody at the ocean thinks, "Did I bring my phone charger?"

Not at the ocean. At the ocean, the focus shifts from me to life . . . and to the one who made all of the life.

Standing and staring at the ocean, I could hear a voice deep in my soul saying, "Life is bigger. Stop making it about you." At the ocean, there is a gravitational pull on our hearts to say, "It's not about me." Each wave is a movement of love coming from somewhere else beyond this earth. All of it points to someone bigger than my questions.

At the ocean, your questions get perspective. Because whoever controls all of this is also watching over me.

The first section of this book is a conversation around three questions I took to the ocean. My hope is these questions will take you to the ocean and lead to more questions and a challenge to love.

Because I think God's love is like the ocean. When you have really experienced the depth of God's love washing over you, it's really hard not to share it with others.

QUESTION #1

WHY DON'T PEOPLE GO TO CHURCH?

Let us think of ways to motivate
one another to acts of love and
good works. And let us not neglect
our meeting together . . .

HEBREWS 10:24-25 NLT

Here is the church. Here is the steeple. Open the door and see all the people.

NURSERY RHYME

QUESTION #1
WHY DON'T PEOPLE GO TO
CHURCH?

The church is people. That's it.
It's that simple.
People on a mission together with Jesus.
That's a church.

The church isn't a building
. . . that's where the church meets.

The church isn't a weekend worship experience
. . . that's when the church gathers for worship.

The church isn't a business.
There is business in a church . . . but that's not all there is. If
it feels like that, then you know something is missing.

The church isn't an impersonal organization
. . . but the body of Christ in this world.

The church isn't just the pastors and priests
. . . they are just there to equip the people to do God's work.

The church is people.

When Jesus started the church, he started with people.
When Jesus launched his mission, he called people to
follow him.

These people became the church. With Jesus. Together.

It seems obvious, right?
But I miss the obvious sometimes.
If you handed someone a Bible, and after they read it you

asked, "What's a church?" what's the chance they would say it is a building, a business, or an institution? I'd say zero.

You can't read the Gospels and get the impression that the church is a building. Why? Because everywhere in the Bible the word church is used, it always refers to people. Every time.

According to the Bible, the church is all of the followers of Jesus
  - throughout history.
  - in the world today.
  - in a city or a region.
  - gathering together for public worship.
  - meeting in a group or in a home.
  - doing life together and sharing resources.

Even the word for church, "ekklesia," refers to people. Ekklesia = called out ones.

Ekklesia was originally used in the Roman Empire, not as a religious word, but referring to an assembly of citizens called out from their homes to a public place for civic purposes. Think a football stadium full of people who have gathered for the good of the city—that's a church.

Ekklesia was also used to refer to a military special forces group with a specific mission. This is Navy SEALs stuff.

However, if you ask someone about a church, they almost always refer to it by the building or the pastor. "Oh, you

mean the church on First Avenue—the one by Dairy Queen—you know, Pastor Wes' church."

Pastor Wes' church . . . huh?

I think Jesus thinks the church belongs to him.

Didn't Jesus say, "I will build my church . . ."?

I tell people if it was Wes' church, I would have a lot more pictures of me all over the place. I can see it now—THE CHURCH OF WES—WESDAVISMINISTRIES.WES—ON THE MISSION WITH WES.

I'm pretty sure I couldn't even get my own family to go to that church.

That's not a church! But can you see why people in our culture could be confused? Even pastors are perplexed.

I sat with a pastor who was trying to start a new church. He showed me his church's mission statement, strategy, core values, branding, and website. Then he asked, "What am I missing?" The only thing I could think of was . . . people.

I said that because that's what we always miss. At least, I did.

When we first launched newlife, there were not a lot of people. I remember getting up, getting dressed, getting my stuff together and then thinking, "I have no idea what I'm doing next." Thank God for coffee shops!

I asked a friend what he thought I should do. He said, "You should probably go meet with people."

If you handed someone
a Bible, and after they
read it you asked:
what's a church?
What's the chance
they would say it's a
building, a business, or a
religious organization.

I'd say Zero.

I thought that sounded like a good idea.

So I made a list of 30 people's names and just started to get together with them.

In the process, I discovered . . .
    I didn't need to launch the church.
        Jesus already did.

I just needed to meet people.

Apparently, I wasn't the only one.

We have a lot of empty church buildings.
    A lot of frustrated pastors.
        A lot of people who "used to go to church."

It's like the old nursery rhyme "Here is the church, here is the steeple . . ." but when we open the doors, we don't see the people.

Where are all the people? Why don't people go to church? Maybe it's because Jesus has bigger plans.

What if Jesus isn't trying to get YOU to go to church? What if Jesus wants you to BECOME the church?

People becoming the church is God's way to change this world because it's the only way that changes you. You become the church. Your friends become the church. Your family becomes the church. Your community becomes the church. You become the church together. That's it. That's you at your full potential.

If that's true, then how does one become the church?

I discovered I didn't
need to launch the church.
Jesus already did. I just needed
to meet people.

QUESTION #2

HOW DO PEOPLE BECOME THE CHURCH?

"Come, follow me,"
- Jesus

MATTHEW 4:18 NIV

Don't let who you were keep
you from who you're
becoming.

BOB GOFF

QUESTION #2
HOW DO PEOPLE
BECOME THE CHURCH?

I'm sure there is a more complex answer to the question of how people become the church, but I just know the easy one.

People become the church the same way people became the church in the New Testament . . . by going on the mission with Jesus.

There is no other way.
There is no other substitute.
You can't become the church by yourself.
You can't become the church in a classroom.
It's impossible.

You can pray by yourself, read the Bible by yourself, and podcast sermons by yourself. But you can't become the church by yourself.

You start to become the church when you start to really follow Jesus with other people who are really following him, too.

That's when everything in your life changes.
At least that's when everything changed for his disciples.
For Simon . . . it even changed his name.

JESUS & NICKNAMES
Did you have a nickname growing up?
One that you liked?

I didn't really have a nickname but I wanted one.

Something cool.

Actually, I almost had a nickname—Dr. Wes.
It wasn't for getting a PhD. It was for being friends with
someone I'll call Dave.

Dave was a student in my high school who was also in the
youth group with me at church. Dave was a one of a kind
individual, and by that I mean a number of students enjoyed
making fun of him. You see, Dave was a student with special
needs. Funny thing is, I don't think he noticed the mocking.
And if he did, he certainly didn't care. He was having too
much fun in life to be slowed down by insults. I can still
see Dave with his red hair, dark-rimmed glasses, and his
tall, skinny frame stuffed inside his favorite brown jacket.
He loved that jacket. I think he wore it every day in high
school—rain, snow, or shine—inside and outside.

For some reason, Dave really liked to call me Dr. Wes.
DOC-TOR WES!
    DOC-TOR WES!
        DOC-TOR WESSSS!

He would shout "Dr. Wes" from the end of the hallway at
Woodrow Wilson High School as he ran toward me, knocking
down students with his red duffel bag carried up high
above his shoulder just to give me a high five.
HIGH FIVE. HIGH FIVE.
HIGH-FIVE, DOC-TOR WES!

I wish I wasn't so insecure about what other people thought
about me in high school because I would really enjoy Dave
today. He was so filled with joy. Such a huge smile. But I was
insecure. It was high school. And I was extremely aware of
social pressure. So I pretty much avoided him whenever I
could and in the process, probably missed out on a really
good nickname. If I ever get my doctorate, I hope Dave is
there so he can call me "DOC-TOR WES!" I can thank him
for believing in me and being the first person to call me Dr.

Nicknames are powerful. Sometimes people get good nicknames.

Jesus nicknamed James and John "Sons of Thunder." That's pretty cool.

Sometimes we get a nickname we don't want. And the worst is when it sticks.
Condolences to "Doubting Thomas."
    I'm sure he would have preferred "Curious Tom."

How do we get nicknames anyway? Usually nicknames come from something that sounds like your name, or what you look like, or something you do (usually, not well). And to get rid of a nickname, you almost have to move or at least change schools.

Names stick. One of the first jobs in the Bible was the job God gave Adam—to name all of the animals. I don't know how many animals there were, but it was probably a really difficult job. You would have to be super creative. It appears that Adam enjoyed that job so much that when he and his wife, Eve, had children they even named them, too. It's such a strong tradition that when my wife and I had kids, we named them, too.

It's a big deal to come up with just the right name for someone you love more than anything else in the world, a name they will have to live with their whole life.

Names are important. Throughout the Bible, when something really big happened—a life-changing moment—God would give someone a new name.

Abram became Abraham
    from noble father to father of many

Sarai became Sarah
>from princess to queen or mother of nations

Jacob became Israel
>from deceiver to one who struggles with God

Even Hosea's children were given new names to reflect God's grace.
>Disaster, Unloved, and Unwanted
>>became Redeemed, Loved, Mine

After losing her husband and sons, Naomi changed her own name to Mara—from beautiful to bitter—before she changed it back after experiencing redemption and God's blessing in her family. Her daughter-in-law is redeemed by Boaz, who would become the great grandfather to a king named David. Somehow she got written into the family tree of the Messiah, Jesus. That really is beautiful.

Daniel was given a new name when he was taken into captivity in the Babylonian exile. His name changed from "God is judge" to Belteshazzar in honor of one of the Babylonian gods, Bel. I bet he didn't like that. However, even though his name was changed, he never forgot his true identity. I think it's interesting that when he wrote the book of Daniel in the Bible, he just kept calling himself by his real name, Daniel. Which is probably good, otherwise we might have a book of the Bible called Belteshazzar.

Saul of Tarsus became the Apostle Paul, which is actually the same name but Saul is Hebrew and Paul is Greek; being called Paul was a reminder of God's calling on his life to take the gospel to the Gentiles and everyone else.

Names are so important we even name hurricanes.

Giving a name to even the painful things in our lives remind us we are human and there is hope that things can change and get better.

Everyone has a name.
You have a name. It's part of who you are.
But Jesus sees not only who you are but who you can become.
I wonder what nickname Jesus has for you.
For Simon, it was Peter.

SIMON PETER

Jesus recruited Simon Peter at least three times to be one of his disciples in the Gospels.
Three times!

Simon's response? *"Oh, Lord, please leave me—I'm such a sinful man" (Luke 5:8, NLT)*

Can you imagine if Jesus would have said, "Okay, I'll pick someone else"? Aren't you glad Jesus sees who we can become?

It also reminds me that sometimes it's the person who says "No" that makes the biggest difference when they finally say "Yes." It's like their "Yes" really means something.

Simon Peter may have never met Jesus had it not been for his brother, Andrew. Seems like God puts an Andrew in all of our lives—someone you trust who introduces you to Jesus. Andrew brought Simon to Jesus; before Simon had a conversation with Jesus, Jesus had already given him a nickname. Like, I know you are Simon, son of John, but I am going to call you Peter.

You are going to become a rock.

BECOMING A ROCK

When Jesus called Simon Peter, he was fishing. That was his trade. He must have been doing a decent job because he was able to take a leave of absence to go on the mission with Jesus. He even hired people in his place to help his dad in their family fishing business.

Simon Peter was a fisherman.
He wasn't a religious leader. But Jesus wasn't looking for religious leaders. And religious leaders weren't looking for Simon Peter.

No rabbi had ever come up to Simon Peter and said, "Follow me."

So after Peter graduated from their version of high school, he went and got a job. He took up the family business.

But Jesus saw something more.
He sees something more in you, too.

Simon finally said "Yes" to following Jesus.
But imagine his surprise when he joined the team of 12 and saw that one of his new teammates used to collect taxes for the enemy, Rome.

Matthew Levi's tax booth was right there in Capernaum, the fishing village of Simon Peter.

Yes, Simon Peter had his brother Andrew and his fishing buddies James and John, but there were people like Matthew Levi and Judas Iscariot, too.

Somehow Jesus knows exactly who Simon needed in his life to become the church. And he knows who you need, too.

It took three years of training.

But Simon became Peter, the first leader of the church.

It definitely looked like Peter failed the final exam when he denied that he even knew Jesus. But even that failure was another opportunity for grace.

The same Simon who asked Jesus, "How many times do we have to forgive someone when they sin against us?" was himself forgiven.

God always seems to do best with people who have experienced the most amount of grace.

Fifty days after failing the final test, Simon stood up on the Day of Pentecost and preached his first sermon . . . and 3,000 people said yes to following Jesus and were baptized.

3,000!
That's a lot of people saying "Yes" to Jesus.

It makes me wonder if sometimes we underestimate what God can do through our obedience. Even the religious leaders noticed something different about Peter when he was arrested and instructed to not preach about Jesus anymore. They couldn't figure out how God could do so much with rather ordinary people.

Maybe ordinary people have advantages over religious leaders.
1.   There are more of them.
2.   They know more people outside the religious bubble.
3.   They are smarter at reaching their tribe.
4.   They are more accustomed to action-based learning and apprenticeship.
5.   Grace looks more obvious in their life.

Jesus saw who Simon was becoming. I think Jesus sees who

you are becoming, too.

". . . you are Peter . . . and upon this rock I will build my church, and all the powers of hell will not conquer it."
(Matthew 16:18, NLT)

I would suggest that Simon would never become Peter by just reading about Jesus. He had to go with Jesus. And we need to go with Jesus, too, if we are going to become who we were always meant to be.

Jesus saw it before anyone else did. Even though he knew Simon would fail. I think God sees past your failures, too.

It's like Jesus is saying, "I've prayed for you . . . I know who you are becoming."

Nobody would have guessed he could preach. But maybe preaching doesn't look so scary after you have walked on the water with Jesus.

Peter becomes a leader in the mission of God and writes these words: *"For God called you to do good, even if it means suffering, just as Christ suffered for you. He is your example, and you must follow in his steps." (1 PETER 2:21 NLT)*

Peter was the first to wear a "What Would Jesus Do?" bracelet and follow in his steps. That is exactly what Peter would do when he was crucified in Rome as a follower of Jesus. He felt it was too much of an honor to be crucified like his Lord so Peter was crucified upside-down. In the process, Peter has inspired hundreds of thousands of people to follow Jesus no matter the cost.

This is people becoming the church.

Simon becomes Peter.

The 12 disciples become world changers.
And you? I don't know what your full kingdom potential is, but I do know you won't find out unless you go on the mission with Jesus and become the church, too.

I wonder what difference that would make.

QUESTION #3

WHAT DIFFERENCE DOES A CHURCH MAKE ANYWAY?

Now I say to you that you are
Peter (which means
'rock'), and upon this rock I
will build my church, and all
the powers of hell will not
conquer it.

– JESUS
(MATTHEW 16:18 NLT)

"The church is not a refuge from the world, but a refuge for the world."

ERWIN MCMANUS

QUESTION #3
WHAT DIFFERENCE DOES A
CHURCH MAKE ANYWAYS?

The church is the largest volunteer workforce in the world.
Nothing is even close.

The church has hundreds of millions of volunteers
everywhere in the world.

They speak every language.
They gather every week.
They are in almost every local community,
with an existing leadership structure in place,
and a myriad of gifts and talents to offer.

Imagine the potential.

Can you see why God's plan to heal the world is through
people becoming the church?

So . . . why isn't it happening more?

If you ask people who aren't going to church, "What's
wrong with the church?" I think they might say "the
Christians." Which is a pretty big problem, since the church
is almost exclusively made up of them. Which makes me
curious. Maybe we have the wrong definition of a Christian.
Have Christians forgot . . . what's a Christian?

WHAT'S A CHRISTIAN?
Who do you think Jesus would call a Christian?
Probably nobody.

Because Jesus never called anyone a Christian. That didn't
happen until about 10 years later. And before Christians
were called Christians, they were called other things. They

had nicknames, too.

Do you know what was one of the first nicknames? "Nazarenes." (See Acts 24:5) Because they followed the teachings of Jesus of Nazareth.

What if that nickname would have stuck?

Can you imagine 2.5 billion people being called Nazarenes today? There would be Nazarene music, Nazarene t-shirts, and even a Nazarene dating website. Before getting married, your Dad might say, "I hope they are a Nazarene . . . a real Nazarene."

Nazarene wasn't exactly a compliment. Saying you were from Nazareth wasn't like a backstage pass into powerful circles. First century Nazareth was a relatively isolated, backwater town with about 400 people and one public bath! This was the high school that didn't have enough boys to field an 8-man football team. Being "straight outta Nazareth" wasn't "street" but "village." It was "pedestrian." And it was so unimpressive that it caused Nathaniel to have second thoughts about following Jesus, saying, "Can anything good come from Nazareth?" (John 1:46, NLT)

Even the people of Nazareth weren't impressed with Jesus. When Jesus returned to preach in the synagogue in Nazareth, they waved him off saying, "He's just a carpenter. The son of Mary." When Jesus kept going, his hometown friends tried to throw him off a cliff.

Calling the followers of Jesus "Nazarenes" was a reminder of how small and insignificant they were in a hugely, Roman-dominated world.

Have you ever felt small or insignificant?

Another nickname was "Followers of the way." Probably because of something Jesus said: *"I am the way, the truth, and the life. No one comes to the Father except through me."* *(John 14:6, NIV)*

That nickname stuck around for a while, too.

This is the nickname Paul called the followers of Jesus before he joined the team. (See Acts 9:2)

Although it doesn't seem too strange to see Jesus is the way on a banner at a football game or on the back of a psychedelic t-shirt, to the ears of a Jewish worshipper, this was scandalous language. The Hebrew Scriptures, or Torah, were "the way" to human flourishing and worship of God.

To the Roman cultured citizen, it was just plain weird. I even wonder if the outsiders who heard these words put "air quotes" around "the way"—like these people are (pause) "way different."

They definitely created some buzz, but there weren't so many "Followers of the Way" that everyone knew one, so most people just had assumptions—things they had heard about them.

This is what happens when you don't actually know people, you just have assumptions.

The common assumptions held about the "Followers of the Way" were:
1. *Antisocial* for not participating in civic festivals. (But to be fair to the Christians, many of these festivals did include lewd behavior, drunkenness, and illicit sex.)
2. *Atheists* for rejecting the pantheon of Roman and Greek gods.

3. *Unpatriotic* for not enthusiastically celebrating the Emperor and Pax Roman. (Instead of saying "Caesar is Lord," they campaigned under the banner "Jesus is Lord".)
4. *Cannibals* for claiming to eat and drink the body and blood of Christ.
5. *Weird* for calling each other brother and sister without being related.
6. *Bad Luck* they were blamed to be the reason for punishment from the gods when disasters struck. (This was a big deal, especially 350 years later when Rome was sacked by Alaric leading St. Augustine to write a defense in his masterpiece *City of God.*)

Antisocial, atheists, unpatriotic, cannibals, weird, and bad luck. That was the stigma of the early church.

It was this . . . and, oh yeah, one more, they really love people a lot, too. "See, they say, how they love one another . . .," is what Tertullian wrote to one of his friends. The "Followers of the Way" were known for the way they loved.

These Jesus people lived so much like Jesus they were ridiculed for it, called "little Christs."

Do you know what the word is for "little Christs"?
Christians.
That nickname really stuck.

These "little Christs" shared everything they had with each other.

They treated outcasts as family.
They even went out into the wilderness and picked up unwanted babies who were left to die of exposure to raise them as their own. (Is this what it means to be pro-life?)

They totally disregarded the social status pecking order of

the Roman world where one-fifth of all citizens were slaves preferring to call each other brother/sister, disciples, and saints. Not only did they treat others as equals, their goal was to become the servant of all.

Look at those "little Christs," people would say. But instead of being offended, the early followers of Jesus were like, "Thank you, that's exactly what we were going for," and adopted the nickname as a compliment. The early church was known for being a lot like Christ.

Question.
Have we lost what it means to be a Christian?
If we've lost it, how do we get it back?

If you want to get back what it means to be a Christian, you have to go back to the first place that people were first called Christians. And for that, you have to go to Antioch.

ANTIOCH CHRISTIANS
The word "Christian" is only used in the Bible three times (twice in Acts and once in 1 Peter.)

The first time the word Christian was used was in Antioch. (See Acts 11:26)

BACK STORY
Barnabas was a leader in the early church. He was sent by the church in Jerusalem to check on an emerging church in Antioch. The gospel was spreading fast. One of the surprising reasons was persecution. People escaping persecution moved to other cities and shared the good news of the gospel as they went.

What was surprising to the church in Jerusalem was that not only were Jews becoming followers of Jesus, but Gentiles, too!

38

What?
Gentiles?
Outsiders?

What are we going to do with all of these outsiders coming into the church? Can Gentiles become Christians without first becoming Jewish?

So they sent Barnabas, a trusted leader, to check on this. Before Barnabas went to Antioch, he stopped off in Tarsus to get Saul.

The irony is that Saul was one of the people persecuting the early church and started this scattering.

As Saul was on his way to have more followers of Jesus put in prison, he had an encounter with Jesus that changed his life forever (and really changed the world). On the Damascus Road, Saul was blinded by a light and a voice calling out to him saying, *"Saul! Saul! Why are you persecuting me?"* *(Acts 9:4, NLT)*

Saul's response, *"Who are you, lord?"* And the voice said, *"I am Jesus, the one you are persecuting!"* *(Acts 9:5, NLT)*

The rest is history.

Saul became a follower of Jesus with a whole new mission in life and went by the name Paul. What a lot of people don't realize is that the early church wasn't so sure about this Saul-Paul being on their team.

Really, I am a follower of Jesus. I'm on your team now.
I thought you would be more excited.

The church in Jerusalem held him at a distance. A bit disillusioned, Saul went to Arabia for a few years before eventually going back to his hometown, Tarsus. It was 12 years between his encounter with Jesus and actually starting his mission. Twelve years! Have you ever felt like you were on the sidelines?

I wonder. What would the world be like if Barnabas hadn't made a pit stop in Tarsus and invited Saul to join him?

Barnabas and Saul went to Antioch.
Antioch became ground zero for the mission of God.

Where the Jerusalem church wanted to protect the gospel and control people, the Antioch church wanted to spread the gospel, launch people, and help heal this world.

At some point, everyone in leadership—whether you are a parent, a business leader, or a pastor—has to face this: You can have control or growth, but you can't have both.

The Jerusalem church chose control and ended up "arrows in." The Antioch church chose growth, went "arrows out," and the gospel message went all over the world.

People like Paul and Barnabas became the church with friends like Silas, Timothy, and John Mark, and met people like Priscilla, Aquila, Lydia, and Luke. These early Christians spread the gospel throughout the Roman empire and changed the world forever. Long after the Caesars had lost power, the gospel was still winning hearts.

For a man named Patrick, living in the fifth century, people becoming the church meant forgiving the barbarians who enslaved him as a boy. Years after his escape home, he got his revenge by returning to Ireland to share the gospel. It is estimated that Patrick and his friends planted a movement of 700 churches among the Celtic people, turning their tribes from war to love. Historian Thomas

Cahill called it "How the Irish Saved Civilization." Apparently, he was not the only one to think it was profound. Because even still, we wear green and celebrate St. Patrick's Day in the western world every March.

For a woman named Mother Teresa, living in 20th century Calcutta, people becoming the church meant caring for the sick and dying. Mother Teresa and her friends gave people dignity to their last breath on earth. I've heard it said that a child wrote her a letter saying I want to do what you do. Her response? "Find your own Calcutta." And because of Mother Teresa and the Sisters of Mercy, a lot of people have found their own Calcutta, too.

Wherever people are becoming the church, the gospel message of hope is healing this world.
Families are restored.
Evil is shutdown.
Businesses get a new bottom line.
Healthcare includes the soul.
Arts inspires love.
Communities spread hope.
This is what happens when people become the church.
Your life has eternal significance.

Have you ever thought about the difference you and your friends could make in the world?

Do you want to take the People Becoming the Church challenge?

It all starts with following Jesus.
It's Jesus-centered.
Action-based.
And we do it together.

So, who wants to go and help heal the world?

SECTION TWO
CHALLENGES

Consider it a sheer gift, friends,
when tests and challenges
come at you from
all sides.

JAMES 1:2 MESSAGE

If it doesn't challenge you, it
won't change you.

FRED DEVITO

CHALLENGES

What's the toughest challenge you have ever overcome in your life? For me, it might have been the Spartan Race.

In retrospect, I really should have watched the promo video or at least looked at one of the pictures on the website. But when your friends want to make a memory together and Groupon has a sale, it's tough to say no.

"It's basically an 8-mile race."

That's what he said.
In this case, he = Brandon.

"You can go as slow as you want and we'll all stay together. It's a team event."

Hmm . . . it would be good to do something as a team. Nothing bonds friends like a shared struggle and overcoming a challenge.

I thought, "I've ran eight miles before. I know I'm not in my top shape. But, we can walk. If it takes two hours, it takes two hours. I can do this."

What I learned was—I can't.
At least not alone.

RACE DAY

Race morning, we met up at the Poulsbo Starbucks, jumped in Brandon's Durango and headed off to Marysville, Wash., for the Super Spartan.

Peter, Tom, Jonathan, John Michael, Brandon, and me.

There were six of us. All friends.
But let's be honest, I was the weakest link.

WILD DOGS

We called our team "Wild Dogs." I heard a training once
about the African wild dog packs. Apparently their kill rate
is the highest percentage in Africa—even better than the lion.
You would think the King of the Jungle would have the best
kill stats, but unlike the lion, wild dogs share leadership,
work in teams, and simply never give up. In other words,
they are too stupid to quit. I think our team name fit.

When we drove up to the race site, I immediately started to
get nervous. First, there was some sort of A-frame climbing
obstacle that looked to be more than 20 feet high. Second, I
saw a rope climb I had failed multiple times in 6th grade.

As we entered the race site, we checked in at registration.
It was there my second red flag went up.

They had us sign a waiver . . . in case we were seriously hurt
or . . . died.

Die? I could die?
You're telling me I could die?
Is this a battle?
Are there real Spartans attacking us?
Is that why it's called the Spartan race?

So I signed the waiver.

In exchange for risking my life, they gave me a t-shirt and a
race chip that kept our time. That felt fair.

Our team was in the last group of starting times, so there
was a bit of a wait. There was an area to practice rope climbing
as well as some of the more technical traversing over obstacles.
Some of the guys wanted to try them. I didn't. No use wearing
yourself out before the race, right?

Instead, I just watched and stretched. Finally, we headed off to the starting line.

CHALLENGES

After a few minutes of hype, pulsing music, and a DJ teaching us the official Spartan chant, the starting gun went off and within a few steps we had our first challenge. It was 4-foot wall. The easiest challenge by far . . . but somehow I banged my shin on the top of the wall and drew blood. Yes, it was a small injury—but nothing was going to stop me.

What I didn't realize was that there would be 29 challenges and it was actually a little longer than the eight miles they put in the brochure. The race took more than four hours!!! Walls, rope climbs, javelin throws, atlas carries, barbed wired crawls the length of football fields, and more burpees than I have ever done in my whole life combined. But the toughest challenge to the Spartan Race was all the mud.

On one climb up the face of a 75-foot mud cliff, I lost my shoe four times! Halfway up the hill, I stepped into a mud pit and my right leg sunk in to my hip. I yelled, "Help!" Brandon looked down at me from the top of the hill and wasn't even tempted to help. To this day, Brandon claims there was no way down to help. He may have been right, since there was a medical team repelling an injured Spartan out to safety.

I yelled long enough that finally the people around me starting digging me out. Sometimes you have to get desperate to get help you need.

Probably the defining moment in the Spartan for me was a 12-foot wall climb. Basically, you jump up off a step, push off the wall, reach for the top of the wall, and pull yourself up and over. It's just that simple . . . for people not built like me.

I couldn't do it. At least not alone.

At one point, Peter was boosting me with both hands on my backside and John Michael was straddling the top of the wall to keep me from tumbling over to my demise. Tom was two obstacles ahead doing his own thing.

I never did get myself over the wall that day, but my friends did. That's when I knew I'd finish.

However, that didn't mean I wouldn't complain. I got really good at complaining. My complaining peaked as I neared the end of the race. It was then that I saw a man with no legs, just arms, propelling himself toward the finish line. All grit— no complaints.

Sometimes you need to see someone else go through a challenge, even more difficult than yours, to see what's possible. He had no legs and I had no excuse. I needed him so I could finish the race right.

Who do you need?
Nobody does the mission alone.

I wasn't alone that day. My teammates pushed me as I pushed myself. Others inspired me as I watched them face challenges. Now, I'm a Spartan and I have the t-shirt and the picture to prove it! Did I tell you there's a medal?
I slept with it.

ON THE MISSION TOGETHER
Jesus knew that everyone was going to need help getting over certain walls in life. That's why we have the church. There were challenges that we would only overcome with encouragement, friendship, and the Holy Spirit. Maybe that's why Jesus never asked anyone to follow him by themselves. The disciples were a team, a pack of wild dogs.

They became the church . . . together.

The rest of this book is about you getting over walls in your life that have been holding you back from your full potential. Really following Jesus isn't just hard—it's impossible . . . by yourself. That is why God gives you the Holy Spirit and your own group of Wild Dogs.

You could read this book by yourself . . . or you and your friends—your family—your coworkers—your classmates— your teammates—your neighbors—your small group— could do it together.

There are 12 challenges in this book.
One each week.

Each chapter is a challenge that is Jesus-centered, action-based discipleship, that you do together. That's *people becoming the church.*

The only question now is: are you going to take the challenge?

50

PEOPLE BECOMING THE CHURCH

CHALLENGE

MY TEAM:

_____

_____

_____

_____

_____

_____

CHALLENGE #1
SAY YES
TO JESUS

FOLLOW JESUS WHEREVER HE LEADS

Then Jesus went to work on his disciples. "Anyone who intends to come with me has to let me lead. You're not in the driver's seat; I am . . .

JESUS
(MATTHEW 16:24 MESSAGE)

I used to think you had to be special for God to use you, but now I know you simply need to say yes.

BOB GOFF

CHALLENGE #1
SAY YES EVERYDAY

Yes is a really big word.
It opens the door to a relationship.

Can I sit here?
Yes.

Want to get a cup of coffee?
Yes.

Are you coming to the party?
Yes.

It all starts with yes.
What if following Jesus is as simple as saying Yes?
Not one time.
But every day.

For a lot of my years as a pastor, I tried to get people to say Yes to Jesus one time so that they would go to heaven when they died. But if you read the Gospels, it seems like Jesus wants you to say Yes everyday so that more of heaven comes here.

Sounds easy. But I have discovered that the hardest part of saying Yes to Jesus every day is saying No to myself. I want to be the center of my universe.

This is the hardest wall to get over. Not because it's the highest, but because it's the first one and it's the key to everything else. If you can get over this wall, you can get over all of them.

It's a lot easier to say yes to yourself. But you will never reach your full potential until you realize this simple truth: it's not about me. Jesus said it this way: *"If any of you wants to be my follower, you must give up your own way, take up your cross, and follow me"* (Matthew 16:24, NLT)

Perhaps the reason why there isn't more heaven on earth is because Christians want Jesus to follow them. At least, that's how it was for me. Let me explain.

THE CENTER OF THE UNIVERSE

Did you know there was a day when people thought the earth was the center of the universe? (Now, I'm not Mr. Science, but I did Wikipedia this.) People thought the earth was the center—and all of our answers and understanding of the stars, the world, and creation was based on that assumption. And some really smart people—Aristotle and Ptolemy—led the way in earth-centered universe thinking.

Everyone was living as if earth was the center of the universe . . . and then one day we find out it's not true. (Shout out to Nicolaus Copernicus, 16th century Polish astronomer. He proposed "The Copernican Model: a sun-centered solar system.) Huh . . . well that changes things.

We had all of the right things—the sun, the moon, the earth, the other planets—but we had them in the wrong order.

Is that you? Can you relate to that?
. . . having the right things in your life but in the wrong order?

Is it possible that we are living with a wrong assumption? Earth-centered living.

Could that be at the root of all of our happiness?
. . . the crux of all the brokenness in our world?

What happens when people live with the assumption that life orbits around them?

Or worse?
What happens when Christians live with an assumption that God orbits around them?

Think about it. The two most common things we say when faced with obstacles:
      1. Doesn't God want me to be happy?
      2. Why is this happening to me?

We are the center of our faith universe.
And it doesn't work.

Does God want me to be happy?
Actually, he has bigger plans.

God's dream for your life is a lot bigger than personal happiness.

God thinks you have the potential to bring joy and real happiness to people all over the place. Turns out that is far more fulfilling. Our lives and our relationships thrive when God is the center and we live to bring him glory. Seeing God smile on your life will be the greatest joy you will ever experience.

You see, God doesn't orbit around us.
It is we who orbit around God and his mission.

Think about the Lord's prayer. It doesn't start with me. It starts with God. "Our Father in heaven."

Before I ask for my daily bread, I pray,
"Your kingdom come, your will be done on earth as it is in heaven." (Matthew 6:10, ESV)

We have it backward and we're getting ripped off.
Life is better when God is bigger.

MINIATURE JESUS

Let me explain it this way. Growing up, I was taught that
when you said Yes to Jesus, it was like inviting Jesus into
your heart. Now, I had never seen my heart, but I had felt
my heartbeat when I pledged allegiance to the American
flag, so I knew where it was.

As a child, I remember being asked if I wanted Jesus to come
live in my heart so I could go to heaven. And though I was
only five, I knew enough at that point that I certainly did
not want to go to hell and that heaven was the preferred
destination. I said Yes. In my mind, I opened the miniature
door to my heart and this miniature Jesus came into my life.
I had invited Jesus into my life. I could prove it. Miniature
Jesus lived inside of me.

From that day forward, Miniature Jesus went everywhere I
went. There were times I sensed he disapproved of where I
was going or what I was doing, and this led to some conflict.
Miniature Jesus and I argued about my decision-making.
And in the end, sometimes I listened and sometimes I didn't.
Even though I didn't always listen, I was always glad he was
there—especially when tempted.

In temptation, I would pray to Miniature Jesus to help
me out, to give me the power to overcome these urges and
desires. In most cases, Miniature Jesus was not quite
powerful enough to keep me from doing what I wanted
to do. Sometimes I felt guilty doing things I knew did not
please him. Other times I thought Miniature Jesus would
just understand.

As I grew older, I asked Miniature Jesus for direction. "What
is your will for my life?" Miniature Jesus rarely answered

me straight out. So, I usually went the way of the first open door and thanked him for the sign. There were times I got the opportunity to share Miniature Jesus with my friends. I was always a little embarrassed talking about him because he was so small. But in the end, I thought they should invite Miniature Jesus into their life, too. It was better than going to hell.

Life with Miniature Jesus was fine. The only problem was he didn't seem real. He also didn't seem powerful enough to change the world—he couldn't even change me.

Is this all there is?
Have you asked that before?
If God is real, shouldn't he be bigger than this?

What I discovered was, he is.
The real Jesus isn't really miniature and he isn't trying to follow me around. The real Jesus is Lord of heaven and earth and he has invited me into his life—on his mission. It's on the mission with Jesus that your life changes, and everything else changes, too.

Jesus invites you into his life, and his life is bigger than yours.

Look. I totally get that the Bible teaches that Jesus lives inside of his followers. He knocks on the door of our heart, we open it up, and he lives inside of us. But it doesn't stop there.

The Bible talks multiple times of Jesus living inside of us:
- Galatians 2:20, NIV—I have been crucified with Christ and I no longer live but Christ lives in me.
- Colossians 1:27, NLT—And this is the secret: Christ lives in you.

- Ephesians 3:17, NLT—Christ will make his home in
  your hearts as you trust in him.
- Revelation 3:20, NLT—I stand at the door and knock.
  If you hear my voice and open the door,
  I will come in.

So, it's true that Christ lives in us.
But, here is what is also true: we live in Christ.

In fact, the overwhelming teaching of the New Testament is
that the followers of Jesus have a new identity and a new life.
It is described in these two words: en Cristos.

We are now . . . in Christ.
It's in the Bible more than 250 times.

EN CRISTOS
- Romans 6:11, NIV—In the same way, count
  yourselves dead to sin but alive to God in Christ Jesus.
- Romans 6:23, NIV—For the wages of sin is death, but
  the gift of God is eternal life in Christ Jesus our Lord.
- Romans 8:1, NIV—Therefore, there is now no
  condemnation for those who are in Christ Jesus.
- Romans 8:39, NLT—Nothing will be able to separate
  us from the love of God that is in Christ Jesus our
  Lord.
- Ephesians 2:10, NLT—For we are God's masterpiece.
  He has created us anew in Christ Jesus
- 2 Corinthians 5:17, NIV—Therefore, if anyone is in
  Christ, he is a new creation; the old has gone, the new
  has come!
- Philippians 3:14, NIV—I press on toward the goal to
  win the prize for which God has called me
  heavenward in Christ Jesus.
- Philippians 4:7, NIV—And the peace of God, which
  transcends all understanding, will guard your hearts
  and your minds in Christ Jesus.

- Philippians 4:19, NIV—And my God will meet all your needs according to his glorious riches in Christ Jesus

Jesus invites us into his life. Not the other way around. At no point did Jesus run up to Peter, James, and John and say, "Hey guys, where are you going? Can I come too?"

Jesus said two words: Follow me. I have found it's the same two words he says to me every day.

THE VOICE OF JESUS

Have you ever heard this: big goals need small habits? If you want to change the world, you probably have to start with changing how you start your day. We have to change our habits. There is one habit that will change everything in your day and that is listening for the voice of Jesus.

Jesus said, *"My sheep know my voice. I know them, and they follow me." (John 10:27, NLT)*

That's a follower of Jesus.
How else can you follow if you can't hear his voice.
Communication is crucial.

I used to think either God wasn't really good at communication or he wasn't really interested in speaking to me. Now, I realize I was just too distracted. Are you too distracted, too?

Our world is really loud. There is sound everywhere. There is so much noise that there is actually something called noise pollution. (And I'm not talking about country music.) There is excessive noise that disrupts our lives, which is interesting because the word for noise is derived from the Latin word meaning "seasickness." Maybe that is why the Bible says, "Be still, and know that I am God!" (Psalm 46:10, NLT)

62

Maybe God does want to speak to me.
I just need to become a better listener. And I need better reception.

Two things I've noticed about my cell phone: it doesn't work when my battery is dead, and even when it's charged, I can't use it when I don't have good cell reception.

I think it's like that with prayer.
When my spiritual batteries aren't charged up, I don't hear the voice of Jesus.

Four things that keep my spiritual batteries charged are:
1. Prayer
2. The Bible
3. The Church
4. Rest

But even when my soul is refueled, I have to be in a place that I get good coverage. Maybe that's why Jesus said: *"But when you pray, go away by yourself, shut the door behind you, and pray to your Father in private." (Matthew 6:6, NLT)*

The first time I did this I actually went into the closet in my bedroom. I sat there for a while, but I didn't hear anything. Eventually I got hungry so I opened the door and got something to eat. I thought maybe I did it wrong. But then I read that Jesus said to pray you simply have to be yourself and let the attention shift from you to God. That is when you begin to feel his presence.

So the next time I prayed alone, I stopped thinking about me.
That went a lot better.

God speaks more when you stop making it about you.
I guess that's the biggest distraction. Somehow, when we

start the day with a strong connection to God, we hear the voice of Jesus all through the day.

JESUS, IS THAT YOU?

I think it's important to lay some ground rules here for God speaking that will protect you and protect others. You know, the whole subject of God speaking can be scary to some because they have seen what happens when someone uses it to manipulate others.

Three simple rules of thumb I have found are:

1. Does this line up with what Jesus said in the Bible? If Jesus is the Word of God (John 1:14) and if all Scripture points to Jesus (John 5:39), then you can look to Jesus to see if it's really God. This is also why I like to read the Gospels—the life and teaching of Jesus—over and over. It helps me throw stuff out that isn't Jesus.

2. Does this line up with what Jesus teaches about love? If it's controlling, then it's not from Jesus because love is a choice. So someone could say, "God told me to tell you" and it could be God, but it also could be manipulation. If it sounds controlling and it's isolating you from people who love you, then I think you can say to them, "God told me to tell you no."

3. Does this sound weird? If so, you should bounce this off someone else. It's one of the reasons why we go on the mission together. Because if we are left alone long enough we could all become Tom Hanks in Castaway with a weird attachment to a volleyball named Wilson. God is supernatural, but he isn't super-weird.
Reading the Bible, it seems like God didn't have any trouble speaking to people. The hard part was getting them to do what he says. That's the hard part with me, too.

YES, EVERY DAY

What if this week you practiced a new habit?
What if you listened for the voice of Jesus and said Yes every day to whatever Jesus asked you to do?

This is the first challenge of people becoming the church— saying Yes to Jesus every day. This is how your whole life becomes a mission with Jesus.

I wonder what would happen if everyone did this?
I wonder what would happen in your life? In your family? In your community?

Let's find out.

CHALLENGE #1
SAY YES
EVERY DAY

Simple Steps:

1. Start your day centered on God.

       Time: _____

       Place: _____

2. Read something from the Bible.

3. Ask Jesus, "What are you saying to me?"

4. Do it.

5. Talk about what happens with your group.

TALK ABOUT IT

GROUP QUESTIONS

1. Jesus can seem so small—"miniature"—if we think we are only "inviting Him into our hearts." What would change in your life as you realize you are instead "in Christ?"

2. Hearing the voice of Jesus requires our spiritual batteries be fully charged. Which of the crucial practices—page 62—allow you to hear the voice of Jesus? Which practices are a challenge for you?

3. Why do we want to read the Gospels over and over again? Why do the Gospel writers insist we start with the life of Jesus?

CHALLENGE #2
TEAMMATE
NOBODY DOES THE MISSION ALONE

They committed
themselves to the
teaching of the apostles,
the life together, the
common meal,
and the prayers.

THE EARLY CHURCH
(ACTS 2:42 MESSAGE)

As iron sharpens
iron, so a friend sharpens a
friend.

PROVERBS 27:17 NLT

CHALLENGE #2
TEAMMATES

There are a lot of things you can do by yourself, but
following Jesus isn't one of them.

You can read a book by yourself.
Eat a meal by yourself.
Watch a movie by yourself.
Even shoot baskets by yourself.
But you can't follow Jesus by yourself.

Which reminds me of the movie Hoosiers. It's a story about a
small town high school basketball team from Hickory, Ind.
Everyone is passionate about basketball, but the best player
in town doesn't want to play on the team.

Basketball prodigy Jimmy Chitwood spends the first part
of the movie shooting baskets by himself as the whole town
pressures him to play. It seems like Jimmy thinks the only
thing worse than shooting baskets by yourself is being on a
self-absorbed team.

I wonder if there are a lot of Jimmy Chitwoods in the
world—people who love Jesus but aren't sure they want to
be on the church team.

Ironically, it isn't someone perfect who gets Jimmy
to play—it's someone authentic.

Coach Norman Dale has a flawed past, but he's honest about
it. Even though Coach Dale never pressures Jimmy to play
on the team, eventually Jimmy decides to be on the team to
save the coach's job.

Along the way, what starts off being a story about basketball becomes one about friendship and love.

Jesus knew the church is about more than religious people going to weekend gatherings. It's about love. Jesus offered people around him something better than shooting baskets by themselves.

Jesus gave people a chance to become teammates
. . . to go on a mission together
. . . to support each other
. . . and to experience something along the way—real love.

Because nobody does the mission alone.
Not even Jesus.

THINGS YOU CAN'T LEARN BY YOURSELF
One thing you can't learn by yourself is how to love.
Try it. You can't.
There is no way to learn to love by yourself.

Love takes people. Plural.
And learning to love is the most important lesson in life.

You learn to love in community.
Even God lives in community—a holy community—Father, Son, and Holy Spirit. The reason why you learn to love in community is because you learn to love by being loved. That's how God taught the world to love—he sent Jesus.

The way you show you have received God's love is by loving someone else in Jesus' name. You can't do this by yourself either. This is why Jesus wants people to become the church. It's the proof.

Jesus said: *"Your love for one another will prove to the world that you are my disciples." JOHN 13:35 NLT*

The best proof that Jesus is real in our community is the way we love each other. Not how many baskets you can make in a row, by yourself.

Another thing you can't do by yourself is grow into your full potential.

When you first say yes to following Jesus, you're like a spiritual baby. It's fun. Everyone is excited for you. "Oh that's so cute— they just swore in their prayer." But the hope is that you grow up. When kids are babies, you feed them, hold them, love them, and change their diapers. It's awesome. But it won't be awesome if it's the same thing 10 years later.

To grow into our full potential, we have to grow up.

Over time, we grow from being spiritual children to spiritual adults and spiritual parents. In fact, you will grow up the most when you are helping someone else grow. You have to get involved. Stop shooting baskets by yourself and join the team.

Proverbs says it this way, *"As iron sharpens iron, so a friend sharpens a friend." (Proverbs 27:17, NLT)*

Who sharpens you?
Who are you sharpening?
That's your cohort. That's teammates.

How do we sharpen one another? Speaking the truth in love.

You will never grow into your full potential without hearing hard things from other people. It helps you grow. And you need a lot of trust to hear that much truth.

Another way we sharpen one another is through sacrifice. You give things up, not because they are wrong but because they are getting in the way of your growth or they are getting in the way of someone else's growth.

The Apostle Paul wrote about this in the great love chapter—*When I was a child, I spoke and thought and reasoned as a child. But when I grew up, I put away childish things. (1 Corinthians 13, NLT)*

What do you need to give up to grow?

Probably the quickest way to grow up is responsibility. And you can't do that by yourself either.

Holding my first born in the hospital, I knew it was grow up time.

I think that's when I wrote my first family budget. Carrying the weight of a job and finances to help someone else grow up, this is how I grew up. Now ask me if it was worth it? Absolutely. Nothing has been more worth it.

You can't grow to your full potential without responsibility and you can't grow to your Kingdom potential without carrying some spiritual weight. Where are you involved that the church is counting on you?

Jesus wants you to grow into your full potential so he wants to give you some friends. He wants to give you a spiritual family. Jesus wants to give you an opportunity to be one of the 12 disciples.

JESUS AND THE 12
When Jesus choose his first 12 disciples—his first group of wild dogs—some of them were already friends, some of them were actually family, but some of them would have

never picked each other. That's how you know you're on the right team—a couple of friends, some family, and a couple of new faces.

Jesus saw Andrew and John following him around one day, so he turned around and said, "What do you want?"

Apparently, they just wanted to get to know him better. So Jesus had them come over to his house.

I love that Jesus had people over! We don't really know if it was his house in Capernaum or just a house he was staying in, but we do know that Jesus let John and Andrew lean in and get to know him. I guess you could say Jesus let people belong before they believed.

Later, Andrew was so excited he went and brought Simon Peter to meet Jesus—which is something Andrew made a habit of doing. Every time you read about Andrew in the Gospels, he is bringing someone else to meet Jesus. Do you know someone like that?

Peter and Andrew must have thought of someone else who needed to meet Jesus because the next day Jesus went to Bethsaida (Peter and Andrew's hometown) and looked up Philip.

Philip got so excited that he went and got his friend Nathanael who actually did not seem to really want to meet Jesus. But Philip just said, "Come and see." Later, Philip must have been able to say to Nathanael, "I was right," because Nathanael's impression of Jesus changed the moment he met him.

I think that happens a lot. Some people have a wrong impression of Jesus until they meet him.

Simon and Matthew both had a father with the name Alphaeus.

We don't know if it was the same guy, but it would be pretty ironic because Simon was a zealot and Matthew Levi was a tax collector. And zealots and tax collectors got along about as well as liberals and conservatives.

Thomas was nicknamed "The Twin." Some theologians thought it was because he looked just like Jesus. Which is interesting, because he was the one who doubted Jesus had risen from the dead. Church history says Thomas is the one who took the gospel to India. Not bad for a skeptic.

We don't know a lot about Jude. Other than he was also called Judas and Thaddeus. I think he would pick Jude or Thaddeus after what happened with Judas Iscariot.

Let's talk about Judas Iscariot. I'm not sure how Jesus could pick a disciple who he knew would later betray him. I think that says a lot about Jesus. It also says something about how I view grace.

Perhaps if Jesus could forgive Peter for denying him, he could probably have forgiven Judas, too. But Judas couldn't seem to forgive himself. My point is that these were real people. Not super religious people.

They were not pastors and priests when they began to follow Jesus. They were just people. People becoming the church. I think Jesus wants to give you teammates, too.

If you want to meet people like this, you can go to a church gathering, or you can just have a meal.

JESUS AND FOOD

Food brings people together.
At least when Jesus is at the table.
(Food and, I think, coffee.)

It seems like Jesus' strategy for getting people together was a meal.

Seriously. Read the gospel of Luke. Jesus seems to always be at a meal, on the way to a meal, or coming from a meal. Everything is less awkward when you can take a drink or a bite of something and chew.

Eating was expected.
But who Jesus ate with was unexpected.

It was normal for Jesus (as a travelling, translocal teacher) to teach disciples in town, but it was not normal to have a large crowd (that could threaten the establishment) and it really wasn't normal for a rabbi to eat with a tax collector like Matthew Levi, let alone go to one of his dinner parties. It's like Jesus didn't know the established rules of the first century lunch room.

THE ESTABLISHMENT

Let's start with the Caesar, leader of the Roman Empire. Tiberius Caesar was the stepson of Caesar Augustus (formerly known as Octavian). Octavian was adopted by Julius Caesar and won the throne after a brutal civil war. So you have Julius Caesar deified, Caesar Augustus entitled the son of god, and now Tiberius Caesar who was ruling when Jesus launched his public ministry.

Now, how did Rome rule over their conquered nations? Rome allowed puppet kings to rule the land as a way to keep the peace from a distance. Thus, Herod the Great—the ironic/half-Jewish/puppet King in place when Jesus was born—ruled first-century Palestine. Upon his death, Rome decided to split up his kingdom among his sons. In the region Jesus lived, Herod Antipas was on the throne. He will become famous for his role in John the Baptist's beheading and the crucifixion of Jesus.

Caesar. Herod. Next—Pilate.

To make sure things went Rome's way, they installed a governor in each region. In this region, the governor was **Pontius Pilate**. Let's call him "the babysitter." His big job was to keep the peace and make sure they collected the taxes. The money was needed to continue to provide safety, transportation, education, clean water, and a strong military. In other words, it was needed to stay in charge. It was a capital offense to not pay your taxes. So, in a way, Matthew Levi worked for Pilate.

To make matters more complicated, the Jewish people had a ruling religious council to enforce God's law, called the Sanhedrin, made up of conservatives and liberals— Pharisees and Sadducees. The chief priest led this group, which was responsible for making sure the people of God didn't break God's law. The result was even more rules.

And, of course, there were fights over how to keep those rules and what the real rules were. If you were to buy a book in first century Palestine, it probably wasn't about how to love God with your whole life or how to share God's message with your neighbor; it was probably about one of the big three rules and the best way to keep it.

What were the big three?
Sabbath keeping, circumcision, and dietary law.

So imagine the controversy that Jesus caused when he—a rabbi—ate a meal with the tax collector Matthew Levi and his friends at Matthew's house.

THE LORD'S TABLE

First of all, why are there rules about what to eat and who to eat with? There is actually a really good reason why. Behind the rules for eating practice and dietary law was the clear calling for the people of God to live as a holy community worshipping a holy God. You are to be different.

In addition to that, there are some of the practical reasons for the dietary law in Leviticus. For example, we've got two million people to keep healthy as they travel in the exodus out of slavery and into the Promised Land. Do you have any better ideas?

The problem wasn't that the people of God had convictions about what would be healthy to eat. (You probably have food convictions, too. Gluten-free. No dairy.) The problem was that the convictions became absolutes that separated them from the very people with whom God called them to share the gospel. They forgot the why behind the what. Traditions are good until we forget the why. Instead of sharing God's holiness, the people of God became hyper-focused on protecting God's holiness.

In the New Testament times, who you ate with/shared a table with/invited to your table told others what kind of a person you were. Period. No exceptions. So a religious person would NEVER invite anyone other than a similarly religious person to their table. Any hint of impurity or scandal must be avoided. Purity. Holiness. Ritual contamination from impure people who didn't follow Torah, this was an outward boundary marker for what made up Jewish ritual holiness.

To make matters worse, this was a shame/honor culture. You (and your family!) could be culturally shamed if the wrong person was invited to your table fellowship. News traveled fast. The rest of the lunch room would know. Conversely, honor would be attached to inviting religiously observant people to your table.

And finally, stacked on top, there were political overtones to who you ate with. Rome and her collaborators within the Jewish world (both religious elite and tax-collectors) were to be avoided due to their cultural contamination.

Can you see how everyone, absolutely everyone, only ate at the table with people who were like them? This isn't that different from your high school lunch room.

Who is going to teach the world to love?
Everyone has favorites.
Everyone has people they eat with and people they don't.
Here is what Jesus does. Jesus changes who you eat with.
Jesus teaches you to love.
How does he do it?
Jesus does this at the Lord's Table with a meal.
Jesus breaks the rules and brings people together.
Jesus didn't act like God's holiness needed to be protected.
Jesus acted like God's holiness was contagious. Jesus ate meals with people who felt like outsiders and they became friends.

Jesus thought meals were so powerful that he described coming into someone's life was like eating a meal together (Revelation 3:20).

It makes sense, then, that Jesus, at the end of his mission, gathers disciples to a table. The Lord's Table.

It's here that Jesus took the bread and said *this is my body, which is given for you. (Luke 22:19, NLT)* And he gave it to his disciples.

Jesus took the cup and said *this cup is the new covenant in my blood, which is poured out for you. (Luke 22:20, NIV)*

It's at this Table that the followers of Jesus all over the world (and throughout human history) gather together as teammates with one Lord, one mission, and one church.

Nobody is shooting baskets by themselves. Jesus takes ordinary people, makes them teammates. He teaches them to love.

Who are the unexpected teammates Jesus has brought into your life? How does Jesus want to change your table?

What if you gathered this week in one of your homes and celebrated the Lord's Table? Have a meal with Jesus. Share stories of how you came to follow Jesus and what he is doing in your life.

Eat bread. Drink from the cup.
Pray for each other. And say I'm all in.
Because nobody does the mission alone.

This is the teammate challenge.
Gather weekly around a table with a group of friends and follow Jesus together.

CHALLENGE #2
TEAMMATES

Celebrate the Lord's table
with your friends

Who?

_____

When?

_____

Story?

_____

_____

_____

TALK ABOUT IT

GROUP QUESTIONS

1- Jesus chose real people to be his closest followers. Are you surprised by his choices? What do Jesus' choices of disciples then— mean to you today?

2- Jesus was often on the way to a meal or at a meal. Who you shared a meal with was highly significant in Jesus' culture. Jesus chose unexpected guests to dine with. Who should we invite to a meal? Who would be unexpected today?

3- "You can't grow to your full potential without responsibility and you can't grow to your Kingdom potential without carrying some spiritual weight." Where are you carrying "spiritual weight?" Where could you?

CHALLENGE #3
GOOD
NEIGHBOR
MEET REAL NEEDS IN PRACTICAL WAYS

Love your neighbor
as yourself.

JESUS
(MATTHEW 22:39 NLT)

I see Jesus in every
human being.

MOTHER TERESA

CHALLENGE #3
GOOD NEIGHBOR

What is Jesus up to in your neighborhood?
And how do you find out?

When we launched newlife, I remembered reading John 1:14 in The Message. It said this: *"The Word became flesh and blood, and moved into the neighborhood." (John 1:14, MSG)*

I thought, "Isn't that awesome!"
The incarnation . . . Jesus moved into my neighborhood!

I read that scripture and went around my neighborhood praying for eight weeks. You know what happened? Nothing. At least in my mind, nothing happened. So, I just went on to the next thing.

About six months later, I was filling my wheelbarrow with mulch from the mound of 10 yards that I ordered. It was heavy. As I stopped to take a break, I looked down the cul-de-sac and saw two teenage boys walking up the hill with a basketball. They had just finished a game of one-on-one at the neighborhood hoop.

I shouted out to them, "Hey, you guys want to make some money?"

They said, "Yes." (Because they are Americans)
And I hired them to work with me.

Day two of the job, as I was calculating if I was getting my money's worth out of their efforts, I heard that still, small voice of the Holy Spirit whisper, "Remember when you prayed for your neighbors? Well, here they are."

I froze.

It had been a while since I had talked with a neighbor about God.

So I asked, "Do you guys go to church anywhere?"

The first kid said, "Not right now. But I used to go to a Christian school."

The second kid said, "No. But I went to a Christian daycare for one day. Does that count?" (Of course that counts.)

So I said, "I go to a new church that meets up the hill. I'll make you a deal. I'll play you two-on-one basketball. If I win, you go to church with me."

They said, "What if we win?"

I thought, well, that's not going to happen, but I'll buy you pizza either way.

So we played. I'm six foot five. They aren't. Seven layups later, they were going to church.

That next Sunday, they were in my driveway and we got in the car. They went to a gathering and helped out in another. Then I drove them home. We sat and talked for a while in the car. They told me about their lives and what they were going through. I listened. Then they got out of the car and went inside their homes.

We did that for the next four years.
Then they got their driver's licenses.

We talked about a lot of things in that car over the years.

Sports.
School pressure.
Girlfriends.
Breakups.
Getting back together.
Breakups again.

They both were baptized.
Served with kids.
Had powerful experiences with God at summer camp.
I even got to take one with me to Africa on a mission trip.

I got to see my neighbors become the church.
And I will never forget those Sundays together.

I used to think I had to introduce my neighbors to Jesus.
Now I realize Jesus wants to introduce my neighbors to me.

Does Jesus want to introduce your neighbors to you?

How does he do that?

I discovered it was different than how I thought. It's different in two ways.

First, Jesus expands who we see as a neighbor.

We tend to see our neighbor as someone who is like us.

For the Israelite, their neighbor was a fellow Jew. And "love your neighbor" wasn't something Jesus said, but something that came from Moses in Leviticus.

Do not seek revenge or bear a grudge against a fellow Israelite, but love your neighbor as yourself. I am the LORD.
(Leviticus 19:18 NLT)

I used to think that I had
to introduce my neighbors
to Jesus. Until I discovered that
Jesus wants to
introduce them to me.

This is where "love your neighbor" comes from.
It's part of a longer section, one that gives really practical
ways to be a good neighbor.

Some examples:
- When you harvest, don't harvest everything but leave
  some on the edges for the poor. A good neighbor is
  generous.
- Don't steal, cheat, deceive, or defraud your neighbor.
- If someone works for you, don't hold back their
  wages. Pay them a good wage.
- Don't insult people with special needs.
- Don't show favoritism to the rich.
- Don't spread gossip.
- If your neighbor's life is threatened, do something.
- Don't seek revenge, harbor resentment, or nurse a
  grudge. Rather, love your neighbor.

Love your neighbor was God's way of saying:
    Work hard. Be nice.

The problem is that we want to pick "who" we have to be
nice to.

Leviticus says don't seek revenge on a fellow Israelite but
love your neighbor as yourself. The natural tendency is then
to think this: my neighbor is someone who is on the same
team that I'm on. "Fellow Israelite" must equal my neighbor.
Can you see how this led to an attitude that said love your
neighbor, but hate your enemy?

Jesus confronts this in the Sermon on the Mount. It became
known as "the hate clause." (Ps 139:21-22—Shouldn't I
hate who you hate?). Does God hate people? If so, they're
probably my enemy.

Can you see how we could have a lot of wars and other problems with that thinking?

Jesus says this:
You have heard the law that says, 'Love your neighbor and hate your enemy.' But I say Love your enemies. Pray for those who persecute you! In that way, you will be acting as true children of your Father in heaven. (Matthew 5:43-45 NLT)

Jesus expands our understanding of what it means to be a good neighbor. It includes loving your enemies and praying for those who persecute. That's the bar for a good neighbor.

Jesus literally lives this out. He shows us we are loved by God and that is the love that will heal this world.

Jesus says your neighbor is probably someone "not like you," someone who lives differently, has a different belief in God, they might vote differently than you do. (Getting clearer?) They have a different worldview. They have different ethics, a different view of right and wrong. This, this is your neighbor. Love that person like God loves you.

Your neighbor is probably not the person you love the most, but the person you love the least. That's the neighbor God is calling you to love.

Next, Jesus switches who gets to be the Good Neighbor. He takes the question, "Who is my neighbor?" and gives it a plot twist. He instead asks, "Who has been a neighbor to you?"

In every version I could think of, it ended with me being the Good Neighbor coming to rescue my poor neighbors from their ways. Somehow my version of the story always ended with me as the hero.

Ironically, when Jesus told the story of the Good Neighbor, it sounded different than my version.

Jesus replied with a story: A Jewish man was traveling from Jerusalem down to Jericho, and he was attacked by bandits. They stripped him of his clothes, beat him up, and left him half dead beside the road. By chance, a priest came along. But when he saw the man lying there, he crossed to the other side of the road and passed him by. A temple assistant walked over and looked at him lying there, but he also passed by on the other side. (Luke 10:30-32 NLT)

The road from Jerusalem to Jericho is a 3,300-foot drop in about 17 miles. It was a dangerous road to travel because robbers hid along its steep, winding way.

A priest—one expected to love others—avoids the wounded man, probably a fellow Jew. He is busy. He has important business. If he touches the wounded man, it could make him unclean and unable to fulfill his ministry duties. He may not be able to serve in the temple. This is a risk he is unwilling to take. He passes by.

A temple assistant, assistant to the priest, the Levites, descendants of Levi but not of Aaron (Aaron = priests, Levi = assistants). Maybe they will stop? No.

Our neighbors are in our path on a daily basis. You drive by them. You share a cubicle with them. You are in the same class at school. You sit by them on the ferry. Truth is, it's harder to see our neighbors' hurts today than it is in this story, but all around us are people who are wounded, hurt, and have been beat up by life just as we have. At some point, we have all been broken.

Jesus says imagine you are the one broken.
You aren't the Good Neighbor.
You need a good neighbor.
People see you. Nobody stops.
Then a despised Samaritan came along, and when he saw the man,
he felt compassion for him. LUKE 10:33 NLT

A despised Samaritan. Jesus says it's the person on the
opposing team—they live differently, worship differently,
vote differently—they were once all part of the same nation
but there was a divorce, a family split.

This is Jesus saying your neighbor is your ex-wife, your
stepdad, the boss who fired you. That's your neighbor. And
then Jesus makes you the person in need. And that person
is the one who is a good neighbor to you. Classic Jesus. He
flips the script.

You are the broken one.
God chooses the one you despise to teach you how to love
your neighbor. It's on the cross that we see Jesus is the Good
Neighbor rescuing humanity.

Go and do likewise.
Grace in.
Grace out.

Imagine Jesus moves into your neighborhood.
. . . and rescues you.

Now he asks you to join him in loving the rest of the
neighborhood.

Actually . . . neighborhoods.

I say plural because you probably have more than one.
Your neighborhood is not just where you live; your

neighborhoods are where you live, work, and play.

This is the Good Neighbor challenge.
Walk around your neighborhood and pray.
Let Jesus introduce your neighbors to you.
Give God some time and space and he'll do it!

Get to know your neighbors.
Listen to their stories.
Let them be good neighbors to you.
And watch what God does with that.

It's the incarnation.
Jesus is moving into your neighborhood, too.

CHALLENGE #3
GOOD NEIGHBOR

**List out the neighbors in your life. Who lives around you?
What do they do for a living? Who do you work with?
What do they like to do for fun?**

Put down some names in the squares below and ask God
who He wants to introduce you to.

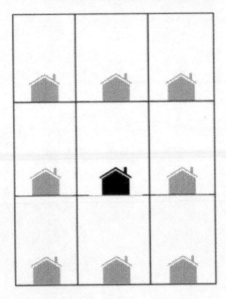

TALK ABOUT IT

GROUP QUESTIONS

1- Jesus is "up to something" in each of our neighborhoods. How do you define "neighbor?" What is Jesus doing in your neighborhood right now? Where do you want Jesus to show up in your neighborhood?

2- Jesus expands our understanding of what it means to be a good neighbor – it includes loving your enemies – praying for those who hurt you. Who is hurting you? Who is your enemy right now? How can you pray for that person today?

3- Who could be/would be a Samaritan in your family? Your community? Your culture? How might God want to use your relationship with that person to bring healing to your neighborhood?

CHALLENGE #4
GOOD NEWS

SHARE GOOD NEWS WITH OTHERS

This Good News tells us
how God makes us right
in his sight.

THE APOSTLE PAUL
ROMANS 1:17 NLT

The gospel is this:
We are more sinful
and flawed in ourselves
than we ever dared believe,
yet at the very same time we are
more loved and accepted
in Jesus Christ than we
ever dared hope.

TIM KELLER

CHALLENGE #4
GOSPEL

What's your story?
I'll tell you mine.

I was born with a cleft lip and a cleft mouth. Very early in my life, I had multiple surgeries. One of my earliest memories was waking up in the hospital and seeing a present from my parents. It was a Sesame Street pillowcase —Big Bird was on one side and Burt & Ernie were on the other. The next memory I had was drinking a milkshake without a straw. It was vanilla. I specifically remember being told I could not use a straw because of the stitches in my mouth. Looking back, my surgeon did a really good job. My cleft lip was noticeable but not overt. There is a small, half-inch scar running diagonally from the center of my nose to just off-center of my mouth. However, it was just enough to draw attention from kids on the playground.

Elementary school was really fun for me. Math, reading, and writing all seemed to come pretty easy for me. The only thing that didn't come easy was pronunciation. As a result of my cleft lip and cleft mouth, I struggled to pronounce certain letters. The toughest (and still are the toughest) were W's and S's—and my parents named me Wes. Seriously. Every introduction was a struggle. And the first part of every new conversation seems to start with, "What's your name?"

Wes.
Russ?

No. Wes.
Les?

Wes.
West?

My name is Wes.
Rust?

I give up.

I can still see the speech therapist standing at the door
calling my name for me to join her in the hallway to
improve my speech. Most of the time, I find people to be
compassionate. But sometimes they can be mean. And that
includes kids.

It was lunch recess in third grade, on the basketball court—
my heaven on earth. Something had gone amiss with the
game. I can't remember. Perhaps it was a disputed score, a
foul that didn't get called, or simply one team had won and
the other team wasn't happy. But something happened that
day that I do remember. One kid grabbed his lip and began
to mock me by slurring his words and mispronouncing my
name. It got to me. Others could tell. So it spread.

It even spread to me. I think that is when I began to make
fun of other people. It deflected the attention away from
me. Of course it hurt them, too. But at least it wasn't me. I
wonder if that is how evil spreads?

It would be some time before I figured out God could use
my words to build people up. And that often our greatest
weaknesses can become a strength when given totally
to God. But that clarity wouldn't happen until later. It
definitely didn't happen on that playground.

It's interesting what we remember. Most likely, my playground
friends do not remember that moment. Because we were

friends. And it was just one lunch recess. An anomaly. It wasn't a defining moment for them. But it was for me. It stung. You remember when someone makes fun of something you can't change, and you remember when someone makes fun of your name.

My name is Wesley Donald Davis, middle name named after my Dad. First name, I'm not sure. I just know that my parents said when I was born, they knew to name me Wesley. The nurse said, "That sounds like a preacher's name" (a.k.a. John Wesley). And in the irony of God, it really did happen. A kid with a cleft lip and cleft mouth grew up to become a public speaker and pastor. I think God likes to do things that way so more people will believe. For me, it was really good news.

THE HISTORY OF GOSPEL
The word Gospel means good news.
In the New Testament, it is the Greek word = euaggelion.
(It's where we get words like evangelist, evangelical, etc.)
It was an explosive word.

Not just something you heard, but something you felt.
Like . . .
        I do!
            It's a boy!
                The Seahawks win the Super Bowl!

Gospel! It wasn't necessarily a religious word, but a political word. The good news of the Roman Empire was Pax Romana, the peace of Rome is spreading to the world.

This is gospel. Right?

Gospel was very Roman.

Julius Caesar, who united the Republic and was deified after his death, was never the Emperor of Rome. That position of power did not exist. But he wanted it to. And for good reason. Look at all the good we can do in the world if we centralize this power!

But absolute power corrupts . . . absolutely. Some others saw this and planned a coup to assassinate Julius Caesar. Among them were Brutus and Cassius. Julius Caesar was assassinated in the Ides of March (44 B.C.) because they did not want him to have sole power.

The result of Caesar's murder was more killing. A civil war emerged from those who had killed Julius Caesar and those who wanted to avenge his death—among them Caesar's adopted son, Octavian, and one of Caesar's childhood friends, Marc Antony. Brutus and Cassius were defeated and now Octavian and Marc Antony became rivals for the same power.

Eventually Octavian won after a crucial battle (in 31 B.C.).

Marc Antony fled for Egypt (hence Cleopatra) and Octavian assumed the throne as the Emperor of Rome with a new name—Caesar Augustus.

Imagine how excited you would be if you sided with Octavian and picked the winner! Word spreads like wildfire – Good News! Gospel! Octavian Caesar has won the battle! He is the savior of the world! Gospel! This changes everything. I wonder what my role will be in his kingdom. I can't wait for the king to return. It would be two years before Octavian would return to the capital.

For two years . . .
> Gospel—the victory has been won.
> Gospel—the king is returning.
> Gospel—peace is coming to the whole world.

What a powerful word in the Roman Empire! The word Gospel was the single most significant way to communicate the contended extension and domination of the Roman Empire, and of the Emperor himself.

Any Roman citizen upon hearing the shout of "Gospel!" would turn expectantly toward the bearer of this "good news" knowing that somewhere, somehow the Emperor and Roman Empire had just experienced victory.

The birth of the Emperor's first born son would be announced with messengers spreading far and wide shouting, "Gospel!"

The announcement of a significant Roman victory would be announced with a heartfelt shout of "Gospel!"

The word "belonged" to the governing elite of the Roman Empire.

It was set apart and utilized to announce the continued superiority of the Roman Empire against all other kingdoms and people groups. The announcement of "Gospel!" in Roman culture was a moment of patriotic fervor. And then those scrappy followers of Jesus began to announce "Gospel!" . . . and the world has never been the same.

The Gospel was about Jesus.
And good news traveled fast.

THE GOSPEL IS ABOUT JESUS
You shall call him Jesus.
That's what the angel told Mary and Joseph.
Don't even worry about coming up with a name. You can check that off the list. His name will be Jesus.

What does his name mean?

Jesus the Christ.

Jesus is Greek for the Hebrew name Joshua.
It means – the Lord saves.
"... *he will save his people from their sins." (Matthew 1:21, NLT)*
Christ wasn't part of his name. (He was probably Jesus of
Nazareth or Jesus, son of Joseph or Jesus Josephson—I made
that one up.) Christ wasn't his middle name or last name; it
was his title. It's the Greek equivalent of Messiah. Messiah
means the chosen one.

Jesus Christ was not only his name but his mission.
The chosen one to save humanity.
From sin. From death. From evil. From destruction.

This is the good news. The good news is about Jesus.
It's no wonder Mark begins his gospel with, *"This is the Good
News about Jesus the Messiah, the Son of God." (Mark 1:1, NLT)*

The good news is not about politics.
The good news is not about religion.
The good news is not about a concept, an idea, or some very
helpful things for your life.

The good news is all about Jesus!

The gospel is about Jesus.
The birth of Jesus.
The life of Jesus.
The death of Jesus.
The resurrection of Jesus.
The ascension of Jesus.
This is about Jesus. Fully human. Fully divine.
God is with us.
The creator of the universe, God, put on a human body.
He walked among us.
This is what it looks like when God is in charge on earth as it

is in heaven. This is how much the Father loves us.

What happened?
He was betrayed, abandoned, denied.
He suffered and died a cruel death of Roman crucifixion that was designed to keep one alive for the longest amount of torture. And he shouted, "FINISHED!" and he died.

Creation wept. The light of the world had just gone dark. The curtain in the temple that separated humanity from God was torn in half. The earth shook. The hardened Roman soldiers, at the foot of the cross, trembled. Surely this man was God!

He was crucified and he was buried. He was dead and gone. But it was not over. Again and again and again. Gospel. Good news would declare a great victory that would start with these four words. "On the third day . . ." On the third day, Christ rose from the dead.

ROSE
It was Good Friday 2014 when one of our beloved newlifers had a heart attack in downtown Seattle. She was rushed to the hospital and put on life support. Her body was cooled down to see if there was any chance that some cells could be restored. It seemed over for her. But then on Easter Sunday, with her husband lying on the hospital bed next to her, Rose woke up.

Something pretty cool happened. As I went to preach, someone received a text behind the stage. And you could hear whispers . . . she's alive.
She's alive!

Rose had risen.
I tell people that there are only two people I know who have died on Good Friday and risen from the dead on Easter.

Jesus and Rose.

You know what is interesting?
Nobody had to ask any of her friends to share the news.
Nobody went to her husband or children and said, "You
should really tell other people that your mom is alive."
Nobody laid out a strategy with talking points for them to
remember to share this good news with others.

There was nothing you could do to stop them from telling
others. And the people who heard the news were so excited
they told others, too.

I guess that's how you can tell if it's really good news or just
okay news. The really good news travels fast. Maybe this is
why the Gospel spread so rapidly throughout the Roman
Empire. People were coming alive with Christ.

DO AND DONE
I had lunch with a wonderful man who I really wanted to
not like.

His ex-wife and daughter are a part of our church—I ended
up liking him anyways, just like his ex-wife and daughter like
him so much.

He seems like a really good guy. But from the first time I met
him, he seemed like someone who looked guilty. So I told
him. "You look like you are trying to pay for your sins."

He was.
He told me stories of being in the war.
It's probably really hard to be in a war and not feel bad
about something.
He actually said, "I hope that by being baptized I can get
into God's good graces."

That's where I got to tell him the really good news.
You can't.

The Gospel is not about something you do. But something that has been done for you.

Tears began to flow down the sides of his face as I read Romans 5 to him:

Therefore, since we have been made right in God's sight by faith, we have peace with God because of what Jesus Christ our Lord has done for us. (Romans 5:1, NLT)

Religion is spelled "D-O."
The gospel is spelled "D-O-N-E."

Jesus was right when he said on the cross, "It is finished."

Everything is different when you believe this good news.
    Instead of guilt,
        there is joy.

Baptism never made anyone right with God.

Religion is spelled "D-O."
The Gospel is spelled
"D-O-N-E."

It's better than that.

Baptism is the celebration that God has made us right
with him through the death, burial, and resurrection of
Jesus Christ.

It's why we go under the water.
We get to come alive with Christ, too!
It's Easter for everyone!

THE GOSPEL IS FOR EVERYONE
Everyone? Yes. Everyone. The Gospel is for everyone.
Not just the people like you or the people you like.
The Gospel is for everyone.

Sharing the Gospel is the privilege of every follower of Jesus.
It's not telling people how to live. It's telling people what
you have found, what you have experienced.

There is a new book out called The Rise of the Nones. (Almost
sounds like the subtitle for the movie Planet of the Apes 5
or Jurassic Park 7). Do you know what is the single fastest
growing religious group in our time? Those who check
the box next to the word "none" on national surveys. In
America, this is 20 percent of the population. People in the
Bible Belt are like, "What are you talking about?" And we're
like, "Welcome to Kitsap."

In Kitsap County, where I live, there are 185,000 people who
are not a part of any church or any religious group. "Come
to church" or "don't you want to be more religious" isn't
going to cut it. Who are you called to? What's so good about
the good news to them?

C.S. Lewis—one of the greatest Christian authors was "one of
the nones" until his friend J.R.R. Tolkien got him curious.
Eventually C.S. said Yes to Jesus because a trusted friend

lived out the gospel in front of him.

I think that is what Jesus was doing—living out the gospel in front of people. Maybe that's why one of his best friends, John, called Jesus the "Word." Because you could read the gospel by just being with Jesus.

THREE NAMES

When I was a kid, I wrote down three names in my Bible— Max, Stan, and Chris. I prayed for them to know God. I'm not sure what difference I made in their lives, but it made a difference in mine just seeing those names.

Awhile back, Max called me and told me that he was baptized as a Christian. I was like—but how? I wasn't even there to help. I guess Jesus wanted me to know he had a lot more people on his team and even sharing the gospel is something we do together.

1 MIN STORY

We make it too complicated. Jesus thinks all of his disciples can share the gospel. All you have to do is share a story. And if that still feels too hard—Jesus has extra power for you to do that.

. . . you will receive power when the Holy Spirit comes upon you. And you will be my witnesses, telling people about me everywhere . . . (Acts 1:8, NLT)

Jesus doesn't need you to judge people.
And he isn't asking you to be his defense attorney.
He doesn't even need you to be the bailiff.

Jesus wants you to be one of his witnesses.

This is the Gospel Challenge.
Simply get your story ready. And Jesus will send people who

need to hear it. All you have to do is be willing to listen to their story first.

What's the good news in your story?
Write it down.

Practice sharing your story with your friends.
And get ready for God to open the door for you to share your story with more people.

Just start with this: This is how the gospel is good news for broken people like me . . .

CHALLENGE #4
GOOD NEWS

My Story
Write out how the gospel is good news in your life
and share it with at least one of your friends this week.

_____

_____

_____

_____

_____

_____

_____

_____

_____

_____

TALK ABOUT IT

GROUP QUESTIONS

1- What are the defining moments in your life to date? What events have made you the person you are today? Do you see Jesus or the Gospel in your defining moments?

2- The Gospel is not about something you do—but something that has been done for you. Where do you struggle to embrace DONE rather than DO?

3- Where do you need to see the Gospel win in your life?

CHALLENGE #5
GENEROSITY

LIVE A GENEROUS LIFE

The generous will prosper;
those who refresh others will
themselves be refreshed.

(PROVERBS 11:25 NLT)

No one ever became
poor by giving.

ANNE FRANK

CHALLENGE #5
GENEROSITY

The verb of the Bible is give.
God so loved the world that he gave his one and only Son . . .
(John 3:16, NIV)

When God thinks about love, he thinks about giving.
And when God gives, he gives outrageously. He
gives himself.

How would people describe your giving?
Are you generous?

The world we live in says the path to happiness is getting
and consuming, but I think we're getting ripped off. There
are a lot of unhappy people who have a lot of stuff. What
if the path to real happiness and joy is in giving? There is
just nothing like putting a smile on someone's face with an
unexpected gift.

We want to be generous.
So what keeps getting in the way?

You might say it's that you have too many bills, not enough
money, or you'll do it when you have less debt and more in
savings. But generosity always starts with what you have
now, not later. We all have more of something to share.

Have you noticed there isn't a single one of the 10
Commandments that instructs people to give? There isn't.
Not one. But just about all of them command us not to do
the stuff that would keep us from being givers. It's almost like
generosity is the most natural thing to do when our
hearts are in a good place with God.

120

You must not have any other god but me.
You must not make for yourself an idol. (Exodus 20:3-4, NLT)

Idols are what we make when we decide to center our lives
on something or someone other than God. Really, making
idols is simply something we do when we are left alone long
enough to feel the emptiness of our souls.

Stealing, coveting, committing adultery—they're all about
taking. And the irony is, they take away your happiness.

Coveting—wanting something that someone else has—might
be the number one thing that gets in the way of the people of
God becoming more generous.

We want and we want.
But we never have enough to give.
And in the end, are we as happy as we had hoped?

We're getting ripped off.

Maybe that is why Jesus said there is a thief that has come to
steal, kill, and destroy. He knew people were getting ripped
off, too.

The life that Jesus promises is abundant.
Overflowing. Rich and satisfying.
Life that is so full it spills out and blesses others.

And it all starts with God. God is the most outrageous giver.

And when someone gives you something great, you have a
response. It's like you want to give something back. A hug,
a thank you note, a gift in return. I have an assumption that it
is literally wired into us. It's like we can't keep ourselves
from doing it.

Have you seen the Big Bang Theory?
The TV show, of course.

The show revolves around a really smart guy named
Sheldon; he has a super low social IQ and consequently,
interesting interactions with his friends. Sheldon is very
logical, stoic, and he loves Star Trek.

One Christmas, his neighbor Penny gets him a gift. But
before she gives it to him, Sheldon finds out that she got
him a gift. So, he buys a number of gifts of different values
so that he can match the level of gift she got him. If the gift is
okay, she'll get an okay gift, but if it's really nice, she'll
get a really nice gift.

Penny tells him "you don't have to give me a gift," but we
know that is code for, yes, you actually do. Gift giving can
sometimes descend into obligation.

Then something unexpected happens. Penny gives Sheldon
something beyond what he could ever expect—a napkin
used (and signed) by Leonard Nimoy. Yes . . . some of
Spock's DNA.

Sheldon freaks out.
He is overwhelmed and overjoyed
. . . what happens next is priceless.

Sheldon runs out of the room and comes back with
everything he bought, dumps it out all over the room as gifts
to Penny, and still he knows it's not enough. As a last resort,
Sheldon offers Penny the gift that is the hardest for him to give
. . . a hug.

The greatest gift you could ever give is yourself.
God wants you. Your heart. Your affection.
Everything else you give flows out of that.

122

When someone gives you something truly great, it demands a response. We want to give back. That's the power of generosity.

For the follower of Jesus, the heart of generosity is worship. Worship is that moment when we realize that God has given us the greatest gift—the gift of love.

Generosity is the natural overflow of worship.
It connects you to the heart of God.
And it gives God a chance to do something that he really wants to do . . . he wants to bless you.

GOD BLESS YOU!

God bless you! It's usually something you hear after someone sneezes. "God bless you."

I'm not saying we shouldn't do that; it's probably good manners. Especially during cold season. However, I think God wants us to hear it more often. God wants to bless us all the time. And the question isn't if God wants to bless us, but *why*?

Why does God want to bless you?
The obvious reason is because God loves you.
But that's not the only reason.
God blesses you so you can bless others.
It's one of the ways you let people know God loves them, too. God loves to bless.
Seriously. Open up to the beginning of the Bible, Genesis 1.

He is blessing everything all over the place.
God loves to bless.
Everything God makes, he blesses.
God makes a day. And he blessed it.

God makes animals. They get blessed.

And then God makes humans. Blessed.

God takes a day off—the Sabbath—and he blesses that, too.

Even after Adam and Eve rebel against God and have to suffer the consequences of their selfishness, God keeps pursuing them so he can bless them. God is a good father who really wants to bless his kids.

The struggle is never if God wants to bless us.
It's why God blesses us.
And what we do with it.

CONFUSED
One of the earliest communities in the Bible was the people of Babel.

They were really blessed.
What did they want to do with it?
What was their big dream?
Build a tower to the sky and make a name for themselves.

Doesn't that sound like us today?
Building towers. Making names for ourselves.
. . . and at what cost?

God knew the people of Babel were going to get ripped off so he confuses the languages of these builders and they spread out over the earth.

That's what happens.
When we live to bless ourselves, we end up being confused.

God is at work to turn the arrows of our hearts outward so we can say it's not about me. God blesses me so I can bless others—that's the motto of the generous person. But gravity continues to pull the arrows of our heart inward.

Arrows out = generosity. Arrows in = greed.

The Gospel is what breaks the gravitation pull of greed.

ABRAM SAYS *YES*

The big story continues as God calls to a man named
Abram. He says, *"Leave your native country, your relatives,
and your father's family, and go to the land that I will show you."*
(Genesis 12:1, NLT)

Abram says Yes.

There was no Bible to consult, no church to attend, just the
call to go, and Abram's obedience.

God begins to bless Abram, and for years he and his family
prosper. So much so, Abram and his nephew, Lot, start to
run out of room in the land where they've settled. So Abram
and Lot decide to spread out.

Lot takes his family and his herds and goes south to Sodom;
Abram stays where he is to the west. It might have worked
out fine, except that Lot ends up getting caught in the
middle of a political conflict. Four kings from the north come
down and ransack a bunch of cities in the south, including
Sodom. This army captures both the riches and the people of
Sodom and hauls them away, including Lot.

When Abram hears about this, he does exactly what you'd
hope and expect the forefather of Israel and a follower of
God to do: he rescues his nephew. Apparently, he has 318
trained men just hanging out under his command; he takes
his men, chases down these four kings from the north, and
attacks them at night.

Obviously they don't expect this because they had already
beaten their enemy and were on their way home. Abram

defeats Kerdorlaomer's army and then meets with the king of Sodom. They return home with Lot, a bunch of wealth, and prisoners.

And right in the middle of this excitement and family reunion, a man named Melchizedek shows up out of nowhere and blesses Abram. They have a meal together. Melchizedek speaks a blessing over his life. Abram responds with giving Melchizedek a tenth, or a tithe, of all he had recovered in the battle.

This is the first moment in the Bible where someone gives 10 percent as an act of worship. Abram had a Sheldon napkin moment. Have you?

What would it take for you to give 10 percent of your earnings to the mission of God through your local church?

It would probably take a moment like this.
It would have to be a response to God rescuing your life.
Blessing you so you can bless others.

At that point, 10 percent wouldn't feel like a tax for believing in God or just a good thing Christians do. It would be a passion for people to know the love of God who rescued you. People who believe this give outrageously. People who don't believe this . . . don't.

- Jesus pointed out a widow who had that moment and gave God her last two cents. (See Luke 21:1-4)
- Barnabas had one in the books of Acts when he sold some land and gave it all to the mission. (See Acts 4:37)
- The rich, young ruler almost did, but he couldn't quite believe that what he would gain would be more than what he would give. (See Luke 18:18-23)

- Ananias and Sapphira didn't. But they wanted everyone to think they did. That didn't end well for them. But I'll let you read Acts 5 for that.
- My friend Evelyn must have had that moment because she wanted to give so much I went to her family and asked if her givings were okay with them, too. She keeps a journal of how God keeps blessing her with more.
- My friend Reid did, and after becoming a millionaire in the first 40 years of his life, he spent the next 40 giving himself away. Now there are a lot of handicapped children in China who have a home of hope.
- For Luke, a student I know, it was sacrificing the money he was saving for an Xbox.

Giving 10 percent of what you have rightfully earned doesn't make sense unless you have had a Sheldon napkin moment. Because until then, giving feels like another tax instead of an opportunity to be generous.

The 10 percent moment is pretty big, because later God asks Abram to sacrifice his son. And Abram says Yes. That is outrageous. Of course, God doesn't make him go through with it. But instead, Abram learns something in the process:

1. The real God is not angry and doesn't need to be appeased.
2. The real God isn't asking us to pay for our sins; he was going to do that for us. He is the one who gives his son.

The apostle John would write it this way: *"For this is how God loved the world: He gave his one and only Son, so that everyone who believes in him will not perish but have eternal life." (John 3:16, NLT)*

Abram figures it out.

And God keeps blessing him.
So much so that most of the world in one way or another
considers Abram their spiritual father.

I guess God really meant it when he said, *". . . through your
descendants all the nations of the earth will be blessed." (Genesis
22:18, NLT)* And I guess it makes a lot of sense that one of his
descendants would end up being Jesus.

Maybe we don't give because we don't see the impact or we
don't know how much it matters. But generosity has a life of
its own. It just keeps giving and giving.

The generosity challenge is a really big wall, a huge
challenge of faith, but it's so important for you to become the
church. It has everything to do with how you see God. It has
everything to do with how big of an impact you and your
friends are going to make in the world for Jesus.

Start being generous. Give 10 percent. See what God does.

**Because 90 percent + God is always more than
100 percent + you.**

CHALLENGE #5
BE OUTRAGEOUS

One thing God is asking me to sacrifice for the mission:

_____

_____

_____

_____

What would I have to do to become a 10 percent giver?

_____

_____

_____

_____

_____

TALK ABOUT IT

GROUP QUESTIONS

1. God blesses me so I can bless others – that's the motto of the generous person. But gravity continues to pull the arrows of our heart inward. How do you make life "not about you?" How does the Gospel make you a blessing to others?

2. "Giving 10% of what you have rightfully earned doesn't make sense unless you have had a Sheldon napkin moment. Because until then, giving feels like another tax, instead of an opportunity to be outrageous." What does being generous look like to you? Is it giving time? Money? When have you experienced someone's generosity to you? What's holding you back?

3. What does this mean to you: 90 percent + God is always more than 100 percent + you? What do you think God could do with your 10%?

CHALLENGE #6
MERCY
COMMIT TO FORGIVENESS
IN ALL YOUR RELATIONSHIPS

. . . and forgive us our sins, as
we have forgiven those who sin
against us.

FROM THE LORD'S PRAYER
MATTHEW 6:12

Resentment is like
drinking poison and hoping
it will kill your enemies.

NELSON MANDELA

CHALLENGE #6
MERCY

Who is the hardest person for you to forgive?
Probably the person who has hurt you the most.
Maybe someone who used to be close to you.

Everyone has problems forgiving someone.
For some . . . it's forgiving themselves.

When Jesus talked about forgiveness, he didn't mention
people feeling sorry, but rather coming to their senses.
And Jesus never said something was forgotten, but rather
someone was freed.

When Jesus taught on forgiveness he talked about prison
and debts.

It's why Jesus taught his disciples to pray *"Forgive us our
debts, as we also have forgiven our debtors." (Matthew 6:12, NIV)*

Forgiveness frees two people.
And Grace pays the debt.

What does it mean to have a debt?
Have you ever had a debt?
Maybe it was a mortgage, a car payment, a credit card,
or simply an IOU.

Anybody ever get a call from the bank saying, "You
know that debt you owe? Don't worry about it. We're
ripping it up! "

It's never happened to me.

Why? Because we know the rules.

You owe, you pay.

Imagine getting all dressed up, going to the bank, sitting down with the lender, and saying, "You know, I've been thinking about this and I don't want to pay the debt. The payment is hampering my lifestyle and is just kind of depressing. So, I'm not going to pay it back. Is that okay?

No! People who lend money are quite touchy about this kind of thing.

We have a phrase for people on the street who lend money and are determined to get it back. Loan shark. He's a loan shark because the loan shark has got one rule: You owe, you pay.

You owe, you pay. You sin, you pay. That's a debt.

But what happens when you can't pay?
Jesus told a story about that.

". . . the Kingdom of Heaven can be compared to a king who decided to bring his accounts up to date with servants who had borrowed money from him. In the process, one of his debtors was brought in who owed him millions of dollars. He couldn't pay, so his master ordered that he be sold—along with his wife, his children, and everything he owned—to pay the debt." (Matthew 18:23-35, NLT)

This is the story of a king who wanted to settle accounts, and one man owed him a very large debt. Millions. The original language calls the amount of the debt 10,000 talents or about $50 billion (according to Wes math and the price of gold).

What Jesus actually does is take the highest number in use and then make it plural. It's a little like when we say zillion, or something like that. It's a number too high to calculate, like the national debt. Now, already at this point in the story, several things would be very clear to Jesus' listeners.

The first thing that would strike them is: how would a slave come into possession of such riches? Kings in those days were not in the habit of giving national debt-size loans to slaves. This is a king with a generous heart.

Second, the people listening to the story probably thought: this servant is really dumb! What kind of servant would take so much money from a king and blow the whole wad?

Finally, the listeners probably had a collective gulp when Jesus said the King wanted to settle his accounts. This is D-Day. The King is committed to justice and nobody is getting off the hook.

Now, Matthew understood about settled accounts. This is a rare parable in that it's only found in the gospel of Matthew. None of the other gospels have it. I think there's a reason why Matthew liked it. Do you remember what Matthew's job was? He was a tax collector. Tax collectors understand about settling accounts, don't they? Matthew knew what that was about. He'd heard every lame excuse in the book.

So the time comes for the pronouncement of judgment, and the king says, "Sell him, his wife, his children, all they have." This is not an unusual thing. Imprisonment for debt was very common in Jesus' day to prevent escape and to motivate relatives to pay. But here, this debt is unpayable. That means that this man and his wife and children would be sold from one generation to the next because they could never pay it off. End of sentence, next case.

Everyone knows the rules: you owe, you pay. But then it gets interesting. The servant gets desperate; he has nothing to lose. So he goes for broke. He throws up a Hail Mary.

"But the man fell down before his master and begged him, 'Please, be patient with me, and I will pay it all'" (Matthew 18:26, NLT)

Pay everything back?
This is the national debt. What are the odds that this unemployed slave would be able to pay back a gross national product-sized debt? It's a joke. It's not going to happen.

Everyone waits for the axe to fall.

So what happens?
Mercy.

Then his master was filled with pity for him, and he released him and forgave his debt. (Matthew 18:27, NLT)

The king is moved with compassion. He looks at this frightened, selfish, desperate fool, and he's moved with pity. He does two things, and in the original text he does them in this order. First, he releases the man—gives him no prison time, saves his family, frees his children, and gives him back his home. He is released. But then he goes way beyond that. He forgives the debt.

This is one awesome day for this servant!
He has really good news!

The king pays the debt for the servant.
You owe. I pay.
And I give up my right to punish you.

Imagine what happens when this man goes home and sees his wife. She won't lose her home because of his foolishness. He sees his kids. They're not going to spend their lives in prison. They're free. They've got their life back, and they don't even have to pay the debt.

What a great story!

But that is not where the story ends.

The freshly forgiven servant went out and found one of his fellow servants, one who owed him a few thousand – about $3,000 to be exact. This time, he is the one who is owed money. And that fellow servant says precisely the same words to him that he said to the king.

"His fellow servant fell to his knees and begged him, 'Be patient with me, and I will pay it.'" (Matthew 18:29, NLT)

Now Jesus' listeners would expect surely he will do for this man what the king did for him. They knew he would show mercy.

But he doesn't.
No mercy.

Even though he was forgiven an unpayable debt, he wants his $3,000. Instead of an overflow of mercy, there is no compassion. No pity.

He grabbed him—seized him by the throat and began to choke him.

He is angry.

He doesn't want to forgive the debt.

He doesn't even give the man time to pay it off.
He wants to punish him.
So he throws him in prison where the man has no hope. He violates, in every respect, the king who showed him mercy.

The unmerciful servant has never really understood grace.

People of grace believe this about themselves: "I am the biggest debtor I know."

"When some of the other servants saw this, they were very upset. They went to the king and told him everything that had happened." (Matthew 18:31, NLT)

Very upset.
Is this how people feel when Christians struggle to forgive?

The fellow servants of the kingdom are very upset when they see people who claim to be part of a community of grace withholding grace. So they tell the King.

The slave is brought in one more time, but it's a different story this time around. In this interview, there are no tears, no pleadings, no bargains.

"Then the angry king sent the man to prison to be tortured until he had paid his entire debt." (Matthew 18:34, NLT)

I think this is where the listeners think—good. And rightfully so! The unmerciful servant got what he deserved.

But then Jesus pauses . . . and says, *"That's what my heavenly Father will do to you if you refuse to forgive your brothers and sisters from your heart." (Matthew 18:35, NLT)*

Who is the hardest person for you to forgive?
I'm not sure. Maybe you would say yourself.

But I do know the hardest person for God to forgive.
Me, when I don't show mercy.

$3,000
After speaking the Mercy Challenge at a church with multiple gatherings, I recognized a man from one of the

earlier gatherings returning. As he approached, I could see that his face was flush. Something had happened.

"You don't know this, but I have a friendship that has been ruined because the person owes me $3,000," the man said. "Well, after the message, I got a hold of him and I forgave the debt. I told him our friendship was worth more than $3,000."

He was right.

I don't know if his friend will be changed by the mercy he was shown, but I do know this man will be changed forever. And every relationship he has moving forward will be blessed because he got over this wall.

AS
"Forgive us our sins as we have forgiven those who sin against us." (Matthew 6:12, NLT)

The greatest need in the world is forgiveness.
And the person who cannot forgive, cannot be forgiven.
Grace cannot flow through a heart that has been dammed.

This is not to say that what someone else did to you is okay.
You have been sinned against.

You are the victim of someone's sin.
You have some debtors.
Somebody that you thought you could trust hurt you. They were jealous of you or said bad things about you, twisted the truth about you. Somebody in business deliberately cheated you, took advantage of you financially. And they didn't care that it would break your heart. They didn't care.

Somebody in your own family wounded you. A parent belittled you or neglected you or withheld affection when you needed it. A spouse left you or betrayed you. A friend attacked you. Maybe it was somebody in church; maybe it caused you to leave that church or even leave "the church" altogether.

It was evil.
That evil must be stopped.
And forgiveness swallows that evil to prevent it from going further.

We forgive as often . . .
We forgive as much . . .
We forgive as freely . . .
We forgive as those who have been forgiven.

That's what forgiveness is. But what is it not?

Forgiveness is not tolerating bad behavior.
It confronts.
It names the evil.

Forgiveness is not trust.
Grace is free, but trust is earned.

Forgiveness is not reconciliation.

You cannot build on a relationship unless there is a mutually shared understanding of truth and repentance where it's appropriate.

But forgiveness is giving up the right to hurt them back.
Jesus paid it all.

THE FORGIVENESS MEETING
One of my friends was preparing for a forgiveness meeting. A forgiveness meeting is when two people come together, face to face, with the help of spiritual leaders, for the

purpose of forgiving an evil in Jesus' name.

In this case, the evil was adultery.

My friend loves Jesus.
Their spouse had been getting things right with God.
And this meeting has been months in the planning.
Everyone was taking the right steps forward.
But still, there was so much at stake. My friend was
wrestling.

What if the forgiveness meeting doesn't go as planned?
What if I'm not ready to forgive completely?
What if they don't say the right words?
How could I ever trust again?

I wasn't exactly sure what to say.
That's why it was good that there was another pastor
in the room. He said, "What if you gave yourself permission
to practice forgiveness?"

What if you took every day leading up to the forgiveness
meeting and you practiced?

What if you practiced . . .
- Looking at them and seeing the face of Jesus.
- Listening with compassion to their request for mercy.
- And saying the words, "I forgive you in Jesus' name."

Think about the most important things we do in life. We
practice them. Why would we not practice grace?

What if you did this?
Who do you need to forgive?
What if you practiced forgiving them?
Maybe it would make it easier when a face-to-face
moment comes.

Maybe there is a forgiveness meeting in your future.

Don't be afraid to practice this or to ask for help.
It's a really tough wall to get over.
Start with asking the King to have mercy on you.
The grace will flow from there.

This week is the Mercy Challenge.
Who is one person you need to forgive?
Who is one person you need to ask to forgive you?

CHALLENGE #6
MERCY

One person I'm going to forgive:

_____

One person I'm asking to forgive me:

_____

TALK ABOUT IT

GROUP QUESTIONS

1. "Mercy says—you sin, God pays." How and where have you experienced this unearned forgiveness in your life? Share a story.

2. "Forgiveness is not tolerating bad behavior. Forgiveness is not trust. Forgiveness is not reconciliation—but forgiveness is giving up the right to hurt them back." That's a bold statement! What does this statement mean to you? Where have you had the opportunity to "give up the right"?

3. Followers of Jesus practice forgiveness by seeing the face of Jesus in those who have hurt us. What if you did this? Who do you need to forgive? What if you practiced to forgiving them?

CHALLENGE #7
APPRENTICE

BRING SOMEONE WITH YOU

Follow my example,
as I follow the example
of Christ.

APOSTLE PAUL
1 CORINTHIANS 11:1 NIV

. . . whoever believes in me will do the works I have been doing, and they will do even greater things than these, because I am going to the Father.

JESUS

CHALLENGE #7
APPRENTICE

What's the craziest thing Jesus said?
I'm not sure.
But one of them has to be that his disciples would do even greater things than he did. That's just crazy!

Jesus walked on water!
Freed people from evil spirits!
Fed 5,000 with five loaves of bread and two fish!
Raised Lazarus from the dead!
Rose from the dead on the third day!

Greater things than Jesus?
I would have had a lot lower expectations for the disciples.
But not Jesus.
Jesus had great expectations for his apprentices.
And Jesus has great expectations for you.

Jesus did some amazing things on earth.
But as long as Jesus was on earth, he was limited to one human body.

He changed the hearts and lives of all he healed, but he could not humanly get to everyone. Not in one human body. If Jesus had remained on earth, he would have become a bottleneck to what he cared most about—changing people's hearts.

That's why Jesus poured his life into 12 apprentices to change the world by making more apprentices who would make more apprentices to change the world. And when

Jesus ascended to the Father, the mission not only continued but the movement grew. And it's still growing! Why?

Because Jesus knew how to apprentice.
Jesus said follow me, not follow this.
You become more like Jesus by being with him.

This is how you apprentice.
You invite someone to come with you as you follow Jesus.
It's life on life.
    Not a program.
        Not a weekly meeting.
            Not a book.
                But a relationship.

Jesus left his words and sent his spirit to his apprentices.
Instead of one human Jesus walking around with 12
apprentices, Jesus lives through the lives of millions of
apprentices who inspire more apprentices to change
the world.

So, who is coming with you?

WHO ARE YOU BRINGING WITH YOU?
Jesus let people come with him on the mission of God.
And so can you.
Who do you want to bring with you?

Look around.
Who is God putting in your life?

Jesus did not apprentice by chance or by accident. He did
not wait for disciples to choose him. And Jesus did not
randomly ask people to follow, but he prayed all night
before choosing the 12.

Jesus' invitation was a powerful form of acceptance. When
Jesus invited the disciples into his life it gave them the
opportunity to belong before they had to believe.

Jesus took his disciples everywhere.
They ate together.
They did the mission together.
They served together.
They walked together.
They shared the Gospel together.

Jesus understands that most of what we need to learn about God must be "caught" not "taught." And because Jesus invited disciples into his life, they found it natural to do the same thing, too.

Jesus invited John.
John invited Polycarp.
Polycarp invited Irenaeus.
Irenaeus invited Eusebius.
Disciples making disciples.

Who are you bringing with you?
And what do you believe is their full potential?

GREAT EXPECTATIONS
Greater expectations are an important part of apprenticing because it prevents a "dumbing down" effect.

If disciples believe they can never achieve greater things than their teacher, then they will never attempt it. By doing less than their teacher, they will inevitably pass on to the next generation of students a dumbed-down version of what they received, with even lower expectations.

With each generation of disciples, the quality of the disciple and what they do in Jesus' name would have dwindling results. It's a bad way to make disciples (it doesn't even work raising kids).

How do you know if you have low expectations?

SIGNS OF LOW EXPECTATIONS
1. You think you could never leave.
2. You give away tasks not authority.
3. You attempt to shield people from hardships and rescue them from trouble. (This is also known as the "Helicopter Parent.")
4. There is no room for people to fail.
5. People are not allowed to dream out loud without sounding disloyal.
6. People don't get to lead with you in the room.

Jesus didn't shield his disciples from pain, failure, persecution, or loss, and in the process, they came to depend on God for everything.

God doesn't have low expectations for us. We have low expectations for ourselves. Think about it. The two things Jesus thinks all of his disciples will do are the two things people think only pastors are qualified for.

GREAT COMMISSION
I used to think that the mission of being a Christian was to not sin.
Or at least sin less.
Following Jesus was about sin management.
Don't do this. Don't do that.
If you do, see if you can keep people from finding that out.

After all, you're a Christian.
But is that the mission?
Don't sin. Or sin less.
Or is it bigger than that?
Jesus seemed to think the mission had to do with making disciples to help heal the world.

Maybe that's why Western Christianity isn't working.
Christians don't feel like they have the qualifications, the

training, the abilities to:
1. Share the Gospel.
2. Make disciples and baptize them.

Think about who baptizes.
It's usually priests and pastors.
Is that what Jesus had in mind when he sent all of his
disciples to do it?

What do you think?
Have you baptized anyone lately?
You can.
In fact, according to Jesus, you will.

Imagine what that would look like.
What if everyone who called themselves a follower of
Jesus baptized people whose hearts had changed, and they
wanted to go on the mission, too? Do you think that might
make a difference in the world?

Think about how much you would grow if you thought that
was the expectation.

Jesus ties together the baptism and the training.
Think about how this changes you.
You always learn more trying to pass it on.

Maybe that's part of the problem—we don't think anyone is
watching.

Look, there are only two practices that Jesus told his
apprentices to keep doing: one was baptism and the other
was communion.

People becoming the church means doing both.

It's got to get back into the hands of the people of God.

This is how the movement grows.

BAPTISM
Baptism is powerful.
Both for the person being baptized and the one baptizing.

Jesus modeled this.
He was baptized before he launched his public mission
and before he was tempted for 40 days in the desert. Jesus'
baptism was a significant moment in his life where he got to
hear his Father's approval.

"You are my Son, chosen and marked by my love, pride of my life."
(Luke 3:22, MSG)

Everyone needs that moment. And everyone needs to be
part of that moment for someone else.

Peter got to be part of that moment for a lot of people on the
day of Pentecost.

"Change your life. Turn to God and be baptized, each of you, in
the name of Jesus Christ, so your sins are forgiven. . . . That day
about three thousand took him at his word, were baptized and were
signed up." (Acts 2:38-41, MSG)

And the movement continued . . .
- Philip baptized the Ethiopian Eunich.
- The believers in Damascus baptized Saul.
- Peter baptized Cornelius and his friends.
- Paul baptized Lydia and her whole household; a jailer
  and his household; and Crispus and all his friends, too.

The first step in baptizing someone else is being
baptized yourself.

If you have said Yes to Jesus, then that is your next step. Ask

someone who has being teaching you to follow Jesus to join you in the water and baptize you.
If you have been baptized, it's time to invite someone else to go on the mission with Jesus and get baptized, too.

This is the apprentice challenge.
Who are you inviting to come with you as you follow Jesus?
. . . that might be a good question to ask them, too.

CHALLENGE #7
APPRENTICE

Who is apprenticing me?

_____

_____

Who am I helping to apprentice?

_____

_____

Who is the next to be baptized?

_____

_____

FIVE STEPS
TO APPRENTICE
*From Exponential, by Dave & Jon Ferguson

1. I do. You watch. We talk.

2. I do. You help. We talk.

3. You do. I help. We talk.

4. You do. I watch. We talk.

5. You do. Someone else watches.

TALK ABOUT IT

GROUP QUESTIONS

1. Jesus said, "Follow me." Not "Follow this." Who are you bringing with you on the mission?

2. Jesus had high expectations for his disciples. He believed we would do greater things than he did. How have you been guilty of low expectations of others? What potential do you see in those Jesus is calling you to apprentice?

3. How would your relationships change if you recognized that you might baptize others?

CHALLENGE #8
FREEDOM

CHOOSE TO BE FREE

So if the Son sets you free,
you are truly free.

JESUS
JOHN 8:36 NLT

Behind every sin I do
is a lie I believe.

RICK WARREN

CHALLENGE #8
FREEDOM

I used to think "getting saved" was about going to heaven.
Now I know it's about freedom.

Jesus sets people free. Forever.
That's what Jesus does.

I'm not sure why it took so long for me to figure this out.
It's what Jesus said he was going to do when he quoted the
prophet Isaiah as he launched his public ministry.

> *The Spirit of the Sovereign Lord is upon me,*
> *for the Lord has anointed me*
> *to bring good news to the poor.*
> *He has sent me to comfort the brokenhearted*
> *and to proclaim that captives will be released*
> *and prisoners will be freed.*
> *(Isaiah 61:1, NLT)*

Captives released.
Prisoners freed.
Salvation.

Where do you need to be set free?
It may be an addiction, a bad habit, or a painful past.
And what's underneath that thing that's holding you back.
What's deeper? What's at the root?
Jesus wants to set you free from that.

For most of us, the freedom we need isn't external
but internal.

It's in our head. We need to be set free from the thoughts that imprison us and keep us from our full potential.

THE BRAIN

The brain is an amazing thing. There is a lot going on up there. Did you know that your brain can process up to 50 things at once? It's how you can read this, listen to what's going on around you, and still make a list of stuff to do tomorrow.

The typical brain weights about three pounds, yet it uses 20 percent of the body's total energy and oxygen intake. That's a lot of effort. But it's needed because the latest estimates say that you have about 86 billion brain cells. That's a lot of brain power potential!

And it's growing. A baby's brain is 80 percent of the size of an adult brain, and doesn't reach maturity until about the age of 25.

Yet, while your brain may be growing, attention spans aren't. In 2000, the average attention span was 12 seconds. Now it's 8 seconds. That's shorter than the 9-second attention span of the average goldfish.

So, the next time someone stops paying attention to you, start shouting, "Goldfish! Goldfish! Goldfish!"

Hopefully, they will laugh. Which would be no simple task for the brain. Laughing requires activity in five different areas of the brain. Worship is one of the best activities because it activates all of your brain! No wonder our minds are under attack!

You have 50,000-70,000 thoughts per day. It's estimated that in most people 70 percent of these thoughts are negative.

Here's the point: You can't change your life without

changing your thoughts. If you want to live free, you have to replace old lies with real truth. Jesus was right when he said *". . . you will know the truth, and the truth will set you free."(John 8:32, NLT)*

Your freedom starts with your thoughts.

The Apostle Paul said it this way: *Don't copy the behavior and customs of this world, but let God transform you into a new person by changing the way you think. Then you will learn to know God's will for you, which is good and pleasing and perfect. (Romans 12:2 NLT)*

How does God transform you?
. . . by changing the way you think.

In fact, did you know there is a word that means to "rethink your life," to change your mind?

It's one word.

The word = repent.

Did you know that?
That's what it means to rethink your life completely.
Real repentance always leads to freedom!
Because our lives move in the direction of our strongest thoughts. What are your strongest thoughts?

Do you know what the Apostle Paul called your strongest thoughts? Strongholds.

What's a stronghold? It's a pattern of thinking that is so strong it has become second nature.

A stronghold is a castle.

Think of it as the dungeon in a castle. A prison.
You are locked up.
Imprisoned to lies. Lies you believe about others. Lies you believe about yourself.

Lies like . . .
I am alone.
I do not matter.
They will never change.
God could never forgive me.
It's too late.

You have believed these lies for so long you think there is no way out. You're locked up. You're in the dungeon of a castle believing the deception that there is no way out.

But you're wrong.
Jesus has the key to that dungeon.
Jesus sets people free.

Paul writes . . .

For though we live in the world, we do not wage war as the world does. The weapons we fight with are not the weapons of the world. On the contrary, they have divine power to demolish strongholds. We demolish arguments and every pretension that sets itself up against the knowledge of God, and we take captive every thought to make it obedient to Christ.
(2 Corinthians 10:3-5 NIV)

Jesus has the power to set you free.
Jesus can renew your mind.
You are not trapped.
You don't have to live this way anymore.
Do you believe this good news?

JESUS & EVIL SPIRITS

One of the things you can't get away from in the Gospels is that Jesus sent evil spirits out of people's lives. I'm not sure what we would call it today, but back then they called it an evil spirit.

Casting out evil spirits was one of the main things Jesus did.

Jesus preached the gospel.
Healed people.
And sent away evil spirits.
He was setting people free.

One of the unlikely people Jesus set free was a man chained up in a cemetery. I'm not kidding. This is Stephen King stuff.

Jesus and the 12 disciples are getting away and taking a break. After surviving a storm where even the fisherman thought they were going to drown, they hit land, the region of Gerasenes, Gentile country. (Gerasenes is one of the 10 cities of the Decapolis, centers for the Greco-Roman culture.)

They get there and the greeting team is a demon-possessed man chained up in a cemetery. Welcome to Nightmare on Elm Street! The people in that region had tried to restrain this man with chains and shackles, but they weren't strong enough to subdue him.

This guy was scary.
He wandered around the cemetery, howling and cutting himself with sharp stones. He had moved from obsession to oppression to possession.

Evil dehumanizes people.

I'm thinking, if I was one of the 12 disciples, I would vote we get back into the boat and look for another place to vacation.

What do you do when you are faced with evil?
Confronting evil takes a lot of courage.

We try to manage evil.
We try to contain evil.
And that's exactly what the people of Decapolis had tried to do with this man.

So what does Jesus do when he is faced with evil?
He sets people free.

With a shriek, he screamed, "Why are you interfering with me, Jesus, Son of the Most High God? In the name of God, I beg you, don't torture me!" For Jesus had already said to the spirit, "Come out of the man, you evil spirit." MARK 5:7-8 NLT

Jesus faces the evil.
Even asks the evil, "What's your name?"

Did you know evil has a name?

Murder.
Hate.
Depression.
Death.
Unforgiveness.
Alcoholism.
Broken relationships.
Suicide.
Lies.
Adultery.
Addiction.
Negative thoughts.

So many names.

Jesus asked the evil, "What's your name?"

The evil spirits respond by saying, "Legion, because there are many of us inside this man."

I love that Jesus knew this was the name of the evil but it was not the name of the man. Jesus sends the evil spirits away and sets the man free. Powerful. And shocking.

> *"People rushed out to see what had happened. A crowd soon gathered around Jesus, and they saw the man who had been possessed by the legion of demons. He was sitting there fully clothed and perfectly sane." (Mark 5:14-15 NLT)*

The man begs to go with Jesus.
. . . could this be the 13th disciple?

Jesus says no.
Go home. Tell your family.
. . . your freedom will bring freedom to others.
And that is exactly what the man does. He goes home with good news and everyone is excited.

Civil rights legend Rosa Parks once said, *"I would like to be remembered as a person who wanted to be free . . . so other people would be also free."*

I agree. I want to be free so other people can be free, too.

It was said that the day she refused to go to the back of the bus, she had watched a few buses go by wondering if she was going to go through with it.

I think we all watch a few buses go by.

But everything changes when we finally get on that bus to freedom.

MISSION HOUSE

One of my friends got on that bus one day and went to a place called the Mission House to get freedom from the drug addictions that were holding him back. Not only did he get free from that, he got free from everything else that was holding him back.

At some point you have to ask—how much freedom do I want?

He got so much freedom that God rescued his marriage, too. A year or so later they had a baby. Child number two. A beautiful girl. Now a whole family is enjoying freedom.

His freedom inspired another one of my friends to go to the Mission House. He got so much freedom that now he runs a Mission House.

Every time I see someone graduate, I think back to his decision to be set free, his wife's decision to keep her eyes on Jesus and trust the process, and the support from all the people in the church.

Freedom is something that everyone should want to fight for.

Now, his daughter is fighting for other families, too. At our annual State of the Church event, this 9-year-old prayed for God to heal families like he had healed her family and return fathers, just like Jesus had returned her dad. There were a lot of tears of joy that night. Because real freedom feels awesome for everyone.

We all need freedom somewhere.

Where do you need freedom?
　　What habit do you need to break?
　　　　What hurt needs healing?
　　　　　　What hang up is holding you back?
Jesus wants to set you free. So let him!

Truth sets people free.
So feed your mind with truth.
Put the words of Jesus to memory.
Let them get stuck in your head.

Speak the truths of scripture out loud to yourself and to
each other.
Our minds need to hear us speak the truth.
We have to fight for our friends.
Because Jesus has already fought for us and won.

On the cross, Jesus' last word was, "It is finished."
It sounds like three words. But in the Greek, it is just one.
Teleo.

Finished!
You're free.

This is the freedom challenge.
Where do you need Jesus to set you free?

Have the courage to confront it.
Call it by name.
Then walk out of that dungeon in Jesus' name.
And share the good news with your family and friends.

CHALLENGE #8
FREEDOM

What is one thing (habit, hang up, or hurt)
you want to quit?

_____

_____

_____

TALK ABOUT IT

GROUP QUESTIONS

1. Our lives move in the direction of our strongest thoughts. What are some of the thoughts that are like a prison for you that you need to rethink?

2. Jesus' whole ministry life was spent setting people free. How would your freedom help others become free?

3. What are some things you could you do to change what you think about every day? How will you feed your mind with the truth?

YOU ARE NOT WHO THE ENEMY SAYS YOU ARE

A spoken word by Jenni Waldron

The enemy. Proud. Hungry for my defeat.
Convinced me of the silence of God—the distance of Him.
If I cannot hear Him, I cannot see Him, I cannot feel Him, I
cannot claim His power.

Generations of a single lie, a sickness that led mothers to
shelter their children and fathers to give up their dreams,
and people to give in to schemes for fear of never being
strong enough to battle against the lie.

The night. It's cold and long, quiet. We fear the quiet. We
were conditioned to believe it is unbeatable, trained to fill it
with voices and people and pride and our own desires and
. . . the lie.

YOU ARE NOT ENOUGH
YOU ARE ALONE
YOU ARE TOO BROKEN
TOO LONELY
TOO WEAK
TOO INCONVENIENT
TOO FAR GONE

Gone are the days in which your future stood a chance.
Generations of a single lie, building, growing with each truth
left unclaimed.

With each injustice left the same.
With each family cloaked in shame.

The enemy. Do you hear him now?

Has he convinced you of the silence of God, the distance
of Him? If you cannot hear Him, you cannot see Him, you
cannot feel Him, you cannot claim His power.

God's power that breathes life into bones and dust,
That fills the gap of underserved love with trust.
Limbs that don't work are not destined to hurt, as his name,
which moves mountains is spoken into dirt.

And what has been dead and buried and hopeless
Stands resurrected, redeemed, filled with purpose.

You are not who the enemy says you are.
You are not who the enemy says you are.

You are treasured daughter. Resurrected son.
Your life has been claimed by the Risen One.

Lord of the New Story.
Jesus. The hope of glory.

Breathes life into your bones and dust.
He fills the gap in your desire to be loved with trust.
And the broken places in you are not destined to hurt as the
name of Jesus moves mountains around you.

And you, who were dead and buried and hopeless
Now stand resurrected, redeemed, filled with purpose.

You are not who the enemy says you are.

Do not live as a slave when you have been named daughter
or son.

You are free.

CHALLENGE #9
TAKE BACK MONDAY
RECLAIM THE JOY OF WORK

Work willingly at whatever
you do, as though you were
working for the Lord rather
than for people.

APOSTLE PAUL
COLOSSIANS 3:23 NLT

God doesn't need your good work, but your neighbor does.

MARTIN LUTHER

CHALLENGE #9
TAKE BACK MONDAY

What do you think about Mondays?
Do you love it or dread it?
Seems like a lot of people don't like Mondays.

For many people, Monday is the start of the work week.
For students, it's the beginning of the school week.

Do you know anyone who doesn't like their job?
Probably.
Maybe even you?

If you want to know what you think about your job, just think about how you feel about Mondays. Some people think it'll be different when they get older, but those of you who have lived longer, you know that's not necessarily true. If you wonder, "Where did the bad attitude toward Monday start," look back to how you felt about going to school.

If you don't like your Mondays, at some point you will not like your week. If you don't like your week long enough, at some point you won't like your life.

Is this as good as it gets?

BAD MATH
I like what Jon Acuff calls it when you don't like your Mondays —Bad Math.

Do you remember when you would trade a dime for a nickel because it was bigger . . . until you learned it was bad math.

Well, there are a lot of people getting ripped off with
bad math.

Think about what you are saying.

I don't like my Mondays but I'm willing to trade five days
of my life every week because I get two days off. *That's bad
math.*

I willing to trade 50 weeks of my life because I get two
weeks off. *You're getting ripped off.*

Yes, enjoy your vacation. Enjoy your days off. But, what if
you enjoyed your life?

What if instead of getting a new job your job got a new you?
A new outlook on your week.
Mondays matter to God.

GOD LOVES MONDAY
I think God loves Monday.
In Genesis, Monday was the second day of creation.
On Sunday, God created light.
On Monday, God created space.

Monday was the day God separated the skies and the
waters.

It was the day God laid out a canvas he would fill with the
rest of the week.

What canvas do you lay out on Monday?
What if you thought of your week as creating something that
brings or adds life?
What if your Monday had more meaning?
What if your Monday was different?

You can't change your life without changing your week.
It's time to take back Mondays.

TAKE BACK MONDAYS

Monday is the day we get the work week started.
It's our first day of creation.

Whether you realize it or not, you are creative. Because you
were created in the image of God.

*"So God created man in his own image, in the image of God he
created him; male and female he created them. And God blessed
them. And God said to them, 'Be fruitful and multiply and fill
the earth and subdue it, and have dominion over the fish of the sea
and over the birds of the heavens and over every living thing that
moves on the earth.'" (Genesis 1:27-28 ESV)*

Created man in his own image = IMAGO DEI.
Whether you go to church or not, believe in God or not,
consider yourself a good person or not, the image of God is
stamped on your soul.

You are created in the image of God.
That's what makes you so special.
And it changes three things about our work.

1. You create with your work.

Think about it. You have an opportunity to create. You are a
creator. Of course you are . . . who do you think made you?
It's why as a kid you would make things.

Think about your job—don't just think about the tasks—think
about what you are creating. You can create joy in
someone else's life.

It's not just a cup of coffee you sold, it was the opportunity
for someone to connect over a cup of coffee. It's creating

friendships.

You don't just stock shelves. That food nourishes bodies and may provide an opportunity for friends and family to gather around a meal. It's creating a sense of community.

You don't just work at the shipyard. You are part of creating a free space called the United States of America, where people can freely worship together today. It's creating a space for worship.

2. You worship with your work.
God made you with a unique blend of gifts, talents, and personality. God made you. God knew exactly when you would be born, where you would live, and where you would work.

When you put "you" into your work (heart, soul, mind, and strength), and you do it for God's glory, it brings God immense pleasure. God smiles at your work. God takes the work you have created and sticks it on his fridge! You worship God with your work.

3. You find meaning with work.
After God worked, he looked at what he created and said, "This is good." He was satisfied with his work. It's the reason why you feel good when you do a good work. It's hardwired into you.

Work doesn't drain people.
Work without meaning drains people.

It's not digging a ditch.
It's digging a ditch one day and filling it the next.
And do that for the rest of your life.
I know people who feel like they are digging a ditch today that is going to be filled tomorrow.

God wants to add meaning to your work.
The Take Back Mondays Challenge is about adding meaning to your work.

How can you love God and hate Mondays?
God made Monday.
God made you.
I believe God wants to do something really cool this week through your work.

This is one of the most practical ways to be go on the mission with Jesus.

Maybe if God can help you take back Monday, he can help you take back the rest of your week.

How do you take back Mondays?
It starts with having the mind of Christ.
It begins with new beliefs.
Here are five new mindsets for Mondays.

MINDSET #1
MY WORK IS A BLESSING NOT A CURSE.
The very first thing you are going to do every Monday is say, "THANK YOU GOD FOR MY WORK." If you are a student say, "THANK YOU GOD FOR MY SCHOOL!"

Why would you do that? Because you are going to see your work or your schoolwork as a blessing and not a curse.

> *Work willingly at whatever you do, as though you were working for the Lord rather than for people. (Colossians 3:23, NLT)*

Your work is a blessing. Your work is one of the ways you worship God. The story of God starts with God . . . working, creating, and crafting a place for you and me to exist. The word "abad" in the Bible means work, but it is also used

184

for—you ready—worship.

Work and following Jesus are not separate. They are not
compartmentalized into what you do for yourself and what
you do for God. All of life is spiritual. All of life matters.
What if work is worship? What if your workplace has a lot
to do with God's mission in this world?

> *"Work is rearranging the raw material of God's creation in such a
> way that it helps the world in general, and people in particular,
> thrive and flourish." —TIM KELLER*

Those who serve in the police force, you are keeping a whole
country safe. Families sleep well at night because of you.

Those of you who work in the school district, your work is
a blessing. You are raising up world changers. Those of you
who work a trade or construction or in real estate, your work
matters. It is blessing so many other people with great lives
and a roof over their heads. Those of you who are raising
your kids, your work matters so much. You are teaching
children how important family is and how to be followers
of Jesus.

Aren't you grateful for your work? Gratefulness isn't always
natural. You have to be deliberately grateful. When was the
last time you wrote your job a thank you note? Chances are
the answer is "never."

Today, right now, jot down three or four things you are
thankful for at your job. You don't have to give it to anyone,
but sometimes just the simple act can help. Work should
never just be about the paycheck. You're working for your
kids or your spouse or your future. The work you do matters
and sometimes we forget that. If it's hard to get motivated
for work instead get motivated for why you took that job in
the first place.

MINDSET #2
MY WORKPLACE NEEDS
ME WITH A GOOD ATTITUDE.

Choose a good attitude.
I get that this is hard.
But notice I said choose your attitude not change
your attitude.

I can't change my attitude overnight. It took me a long time
for me to develop this attitude; I have 40+ years invested
in this! Changing an attitude takes time, but choosing an
attitude takes five seconds. Your workplace needs you with a
good attitude.

I was talking with the manager of a Caterpillar equipment
store—think forklifts and cool stuff like that. I told him
about this challenge and asked, "What's the number one
thing you look for [when hiring]?" He didn't even blink. A
good attitude. He said he can teach everything else. A good
attitude is something they have to teach themselves. Wow.

What if every Christian had a good attitude?
It could make a really big difference for the mission of God.

Here's why this is important.
Do you know anyone at work who has a bad attitude?
What do you think about them?

Do you think, "That person probably has amazing good
news—Gospel good news—inside their soul! I mean, look at
their attitude. I need what they have!"

No! Nobody does.

Our attitude at work, our attitude at school is of strategic
missional importance in the Kingdom of God. If your
attitude stinks the only ones who will want to be around you

stink too!

As followers of Jesus, we aren't called to have a good attitude or a great attitude. The bar is higher. We are called to have a Jesus Attitude.

You must have the same attitude that Christ Jesus had.
(Philippians 2:5 NLT)

One of the books I read on a recent vacation was called Ideal Team Player. Great book. It's a leadership book. The author tells a story about a construction company. It's a fable to teach us about the qualities of an ideal team player.

What's an ideal team player?
1. Humble. No ego.
2. Hungry. Driven to grow and learn. Self-starter.
3. Smart. People smart. Relationally intelligent. People like working with you.

The book said the number one quality is humility; if you have that, you can learn the others.

I looked up what it means to be humble. The answer: willing to take on lower-level work for the good of the team.

So what destroys a good attitude?
Equality. Thinking things like "that's not fair!" will destroy a good attitude.

So Paul says, have Christ's attitude instead.

Though he was God, he did not think of equality with God as
something to cling to. (Philippians 2:6 NLT)

Ever cling to fairness? Sometimes we look around at others and think that is not fair. A good attitude comes when you elevate others above yourself. When you let go of trying to make everything even and you just live to elevate the people around you, your attitude changes. How can you make their day better? How can you make their job easier? How can you lift their burden?

Privilege. "It's my right!" Fighting for honor, fighting for the best position. The problem is someone will take your spot. So Paul says, have the same attitude of Christ.

Instead, he gave up his divine privileges; he took the humble position of a slave and was born as a human being. (Philippians 2:7 NLT)

A good attitude comes when you serve others, when you work to help other people succeed.

How about. . .

Pride. "I have to be right."
A good attitude comes when you humbly admit you were wrong. Oh that's hard. But Jesus . . .

When he appeared in human form, he humbled himself in obedience to God and died a criminal's death on a cross. (Philippians 2:7-8 NLT)

Humility makes way for ownership of our actions. It's a lot to maintain when you think you have to be perfect. Humility says I am not perfect, I need Jesus, and I need you to help me.

The bottom line is this: It takes years to change an attitude, it takes a moment to choose your attitude. When you choose a good attitude at work, you change the tone of your workplace. Your attitude toward your workplace is your worship and your witness. It tells people what you think about God and what you think about them.

MINDSET #3
MY CURRENT JOB IS DEVELOPMENT
FOR MY DREAM JOB

The third thing you are going to do every single Monday is ask God to help you develop and hone your skills. You are being developed for something big. Did you know that?

Question. Do you spend more time feeling like you need to be discovered or developed?

Many people in a difficult job pray God will give them a new job. But what if instead of getting a new job, God gives you a new heart and a new vision for your current job? What if God's development plan for you is your current job?

Joseph was a young man and leader in the Bible who was given an opportunity that seemed like a mistake, or at the very least, beneath him. However, Joseph learned that one of the greatest gifts God can give you is a season of development in which you are hidden. God grows your character when nobody is looking so when everyone is looking, you have the character to sustain your gifts.

In order for Joseph to govern Egypt one day, God had to work on his character and it began in a job he was given in an unlikely place—prison. Not to mention all the networking opportunities he got . . .

Hidden. God grows your character when nobody is looking so that when everyone is looking you have the character to sustain your gifts. (If Joseph's dream came true at 17, he might be Justin Bieber. Which tells me that at 30, Justin could still be Joseph.)

God didn't make a mistake by putting you in your

current situation.

All of the skills and character you need to do in your dream job are probably waiting to be developed at your current job. Joseph didn't learn to govern Egypt on the job. He learned that as a slave at Potiphar's house.

MINDSET #4
MY WORK ON EARTH IS CONNECTED TO ETERNITY

Not only are you being developed for bigger opportunities on earth, you are being developed for eternity.

Think about this—are there jobs in heaven?
What job will God give you?
What if people in a lower-level job who did their work with passion, excellence, and faithfulness never got promoted on earth because God had a whole section of heaven for them to run? Those who are faithful with little will be given much.

Your job matters for eternity.
I wonder how your work is preparing you for eternity?
How is your work helping other people prepare for eternity?

MINDSET #5
MORE PEOPLE NEED TO SEE GOD'S GLORY

Make the invisible God visible through your work. Let people see God in the way you work. How do I do this? Give 100 percent effort.

So whether you eat or drink, or whatever you do, do it all for the glory of God. (1 Corinthians 10:31 NLT)

This is the Take Back Monday Challenge.
A wall you face every week.
This is where the rubber meets the road.
This is where it gets real.

What if every Monday you say, "God, this week is for you. May someone around me see that you are real because the way I work points to you."

CHALLENGE #9
TAKE BACK
MONDAY

The Pledge

God is my boss
I work for his glory

My work is a blessing
I am called to bless others

My work has eternal significance
and my Mondays belong to God

So I will work hard
Have a good attitude
Look for opportunities to serve
And continue to grow and get better

This Monday
I will bring glory to god with my work

THIS WEEK

MONDAY
☐ Thank God for your workplace

TUESDAY
☐ Encourage one co-worker

WEDNESDAY
☐ Improve one skill

THURSDAY
☐ Pray for each person at your workplace

FRIDAY
☐ Focus on giving 100 percent effort

TALK ABOUT IT

GROUP QUESTIONS

1. What's the hardest thing about Mondays for you?

2. If we create with our work, what are you creating?

3. Read through the 5 MINDSETS again and pick one to meditate on. How can you live out that mindset this week?

CHALLENGE #10
FAMILY

LOVE THE FAMILY YOU HAVE

God decided in advance to adopt us into his own family by bringing us to himself through Jesus Christ. This is what he wanted to do, and it gave him great pleasure.

APOSTLE PAUL
COLOSSIANS 3:23 NLT

The most important
thing in the world is
family and love.

JOHN WOODEN

CHALLENGE #10
FAMILY

How much do you like your family?

How much does your family like you?

A lot of people love their family.
Many have been hurt by their family.
A few wish they had a different family.
There are even some families that are totally broken.

The reality is this: you didn't pick your family, God did.

The family is the first place God thinks you are going
to learn how to love, forgive, and serve one another. It's
training grounds for being in his family.

You see, God created families.
Families were God's idea.

Here is why—it's in a family, it's in relationships, in
the context of true Biblical community that we really
understand and experience the nature and glory of God.
Because triune God exists in perfect community—Father,
Son, and Holy Spirit.

THE NATURE OF GOD IS A FAMILY.
That's the trinity—one God, three persons, one holy family—
Father, Son, and Holy Spirit.

When Jesus was baptized, the spirit descended like a dove
and the Father God from heaven said this is my Son, whom I
love, and in whom I am well pleased. Now that is a family!

After Jesus rose from the dead, he sent his followers on the mission to go make disciples of all nations, to baptize in the name of the Father, Son, and Holy Spirit. God—the Holy Family—was at work in creation. The Father spoke, the Word created, and the Spirit hovered over the waters.

"Then God said, 'Let us make man in our image, after our likeness.'" (Genesis 1:26, NLT)

God IS a family.

You can't understand God by yourself. You understand and experience God in relationship and in community.

It's the reason why the Ten Commandments talk about how we relate to God and each other. It's why Jesus said the Great Commandment was loving God and loving your neighbor. It's why Jesus started the mission with a family of disciples and why the church is a family. God works through relationships.

And I need to say this. There is no perfect family. None. The very **first family** was Adam, Eve, Cain, and Abel. Adam and Eve rebelled against God. Cain killed Abel. Cain spent the rest of his life as a wanderer.

Noah's family. The only ones righteous enough to be spared in the flood . . . yeah . . . Noah (after the flood) plants a vineyard, gets drunk, lays naked in his tent, and his son, Ham, looks on his nakedness. He tells his brothers and Noah wakes up from his stupor and curses him. And these are the good families.

Abraham and Sarah. Yeah, blended family problem with Ishmael and Isaac, and Ishmael gets sent off to boarding school.

Isaac and Rebekah. Yeah, little problem with his twin sons, Esau and Jacob. Just deception, lying and stealing. Jacob runs away from home with his Father's blessing and his brother's birthright.

Jacob. Small snafu with his Uncle Laban and a little wife swap. You work seven years to marry Rachel and wake up from your honeymoon night married to her sister Leah, the one with the weak eyes and a great personality! Jacob's family was perfect . . . except that he loved Joseph more than his other sons.

Joseph. Well, Joseph's brothers almost killed him and sold him into slavery. Oh yeah . . . and went home and told mom and dad he was dead. This is the family God is going to use to heal the world and bring the Messiah here. It's almost as if God is saying, "If I can forgive, heal, and use them, how could I not work in your family?" Many people limit God. They think he can do anything except work in their family.

God's best miracles are saved for families.

When the Bible talks about families or a house, it's a broader definition than what we are used to. The house/family includes immediate family, blended family, extended family, the people you work with or go to school with, and the friends who are closest to you. It is your household or the Greek word oikos.

THE GOSPEL SPREADS
BEST THROUGH FAMLIES.

The gospel spread through families in the New Testament because whole households (oikos) were coming to faith in Jesus and being baptized together. (Acts 11:14, Acts 16:15, Acts 16:31-32, Acts 18:8)

Oikos includes not only your extended/blended family but

the community of people you lived and worked with.

In Acts 10-11, it's a Roman military leader named **Cornelius** who comes to faith in Jesus with his whole household. *(He will tell you how you and everyone in your household can be saved!)*

In Acts 16, it is a businesswoman named **Lydia** and her household that come to faith and are baptized together. (She was baptized along with other members of her household.)

Also in Acts 16, it's the **jailer** and his household that come to faith in Jesus and is baptized. *(Believe in the Lord Jesus and you will be saved, along with everyone in your household.)*

In Acts 18, it was a leader in the synagogue named **Crispus** who came to faith in Jesus and his household is baptized. *(Crispus, the leader of the synagogue, and everyone in his household believed in the Lord.)*

Who is in your oikos? How is God working in and through your relationships? God is a family. God works through families. And God expects us to care for our families.

THE GOSPEL MESSAGE IS
THE REUNITING OF A FAMILY

The story Jesus told to describe God's outrageous love for us was the reuniting a family. (Luke 15, Prodigal Son)

To illustrate the point further, Jesus told them this story: "A man had two sons. The younger son told his father, 'I want my share of your estate now before you die.' So his father agreed to divide his wealth between his sons. "A few days later this younger son packed all his belongings and moved to a distant land, and there he wasted all his money in wild living. About the time his money ran out, a great famine swept over the land, and he began to starve. He persuaded a local farmer to hire him, and the man sent him into his fields to

feed the pigs. The young man became so hungry that even the pods
he was feeding the pigs looked good to him. But no one gave him
anything. (Luke 15:11-16, NLT)

You have to let people hit bottom.
If you don't, their heart doesn't change, your faith doesn't
grow, and you will just have to bail them out again. Some
of you, you'd rather bail them out and you say it's because
you love them. Listen to me—**that's not love**—that's
codependency—that's making it about you. You're still at
the center and when you're at the center, God isn't. That's
not love.

Love lets people hit bottom so God can do his work in their
hearts. And you're getting in the way.
God loves you enough to let you hit bottom.

This story isn't about us waiting for someone else to hit
bottom. What about you? Where's bottom for you? Where
is it that you will stop and say, "Okay, I'm done with this.
I'm not living this way anymore . . ."? Do you know what
the Bible calls that moment? Repentance. It's where you
rethink your life. It's where you take an honest assessment
of your situation.

Let's see . . . this isn't working.

I'm hungry.
    I have nothing.
        I have no resources.
            I don't want to live this way anymore.
                I can't get myself out of this.
                    Bottom.

You have this moment where you see the light and you come
to your senses.

202

*"When he finally came to his senses, he said to himself,
'At home even the hired servants have food enough to spare,
and here I am dying of hunger! I will go home to my father
and say, "Father, I have sinned against both heaven and you,
and I am no longer worthy of being called your son. Please take
me on as a hired servant."'" (Luke 15:17-19 NLT)*

The prodigal son, he's been wasteful and reckless. And
finally he came to his senses. He comes up with a plan to
get himself out of this mess. He comes up with this plan of
becoming a hired servant.

Even the hired servants have food enough to spare, and here
I am dying of hunger. I will beg my father to *take me on as a
hired servant.*

A hired servant was a day laborer.
They are at the lowest level of the employment pipeline.
They are the poor who are looking for work for the day so
they can have what they need for that day.

What he remembers about his father at that moment was he
paid his day laborers more than enough. His father was a
generous man.

Please take me on as a hired servant.

A hired servant was different than a slave.
Slaves lived in the family. They weren't necessarily paid
wages, but you were in the family.

You had food, a home, and all your basic needs taken care of.

A hired servant wasn't in the family.
They didn't have that level of care and support.

He is willing to go back as a hired servant, not a slave, not a son. He didn't get it in the beginning when he'd rather have his share of the inheritance over a close relationship with his dad. And he still doesn't get the relationship that his father wants to have with him.

Please take me on as a hired servant.

The prodigal is thinking the way the people thought in Jesus' day. They would have said, "You know what? If he's really sorry, if he's truly repentant, he'll go back to his father, he'll confess, he'll repent, he'll be humbled, he'll be humiliated, he'll be scorned, he'll be shamed, and that's just and fair because of the way he treated he father. Let's shame him."

And that's what some of us want.
We know we deserve the shame.
Some people spend their entire Christian life in shame.

Please take me on as a hired servant.

It was very important to protect the honor of the paterfamilias—the father—the head of the house. So you go back and you will be shamed and there will be no forgiveness until you have done enough, worked your way back in. And all the self-righteous people, all the religious leaders listening to Jesus' story, would have been totally with him in the story at this point.

Take me on as your hired servant.

The prodigal son knows all of this, but he's so desperate that he's ready to face it. This is bottom for him.

And then Jesus throws into the story a plot twist . . .

The son returns, it's daylight. The village would be full of people going about their daily activities, and the father is

204

looking and looking for his son. Why? Why is he looking for his son? Why?

Because he wants to reach his son before his son reaches the village. He not only wants to initiate the reconciliation, he wants to get there before other people do because the village would be ready to shame him. He is willing to have people say, "What's that father doing?"

The man who has been dishonored now dishonors himself by embracing this wayward boy. This father just doesn't care what others might say, so he's looking. And if you're going to forgive like the Father, you're going to have to never stop looking.

". . . while he was still a long way off, his father saw him coming. Filled with love and compassion, he ran . . ." (Luke 15:20, NLT)

Why did the father run? He was filled with love for his son and he was filled with compassion. This isn't compassion because of what he did or the condition he's in now. No. This father doesn't want his son to experience the walk of shame into the village.

The word here for compassion refers to your intestines, your bowels, your abdomen. The father felt sick to his stomach when he thought about his son doing the walk of shame. Filled with love and compassion . . .

Would you feel this way?

This is the same son who said I want my portion of the estate now before you die. He disowned you. I want my portion of the estate. You were shocked. You were hurt. And it wasn't easy to get it together. You had to liquidate your sheep, your livestock, your land, and other assets. It's not like you could do that quietly. Everyone in the village would know.

Everyone.

Wouldn't it just be easier to say, "That is not my son.
He is dead."

He's filled with love and compassion. Where does this kind
of love come from? Only God. Only God. You never stop
looking. You never stop loving. And you never stop praying.
You never stop praying.

Noblemen of Middle Eastern culture don't run. They don't
do it. And this word here isn't just a word to describe a jog
or some kind of fast walk; it's the word that was used to
describe a race in a stadium, he was in an all-out sprint.

One of the reasons noblemen didn't run was that their
robes went all the way to the ground. No one can run in a
robe without picking it up. Nobody. So how do you run?
You grab the corners of your robe, tie it in a knot (it's called
girding your loins) and you expose your legs. When the legs
would be exposed, that would be a fashion faux pas and it
was considered humiliating.

The Arabic versions of the Bible wouldn't even translate this
word run; all it says is that he went. But the word Jesus used
was an Usain Bolt sprint. He doesn't worry about his rights,
his pride, his honor; he brings shame on himself so his son
doesn't have to carry all the shame.

*". . . filled with love and compassion, he ran to his son, embraced
him, and kissed him." (Luke 15:20, NLT)*

The word use for kissed here is a word that means "to kiss
repeatedly." Think about the irony. In a culture where the
son was expected to kiss his feet, the father is kissing his
son's head. This is the kiss of acceptance, love, forgiveness,
and reconciliation. And it's a shock to the son and a scandal

to the listeners of the story because this all happens without
the son earning it back.

The son is so shocked that he leaves out the whole part of his
speech about becoming a hired servant. He just says, "Father,
I have sinned against both heaven and you, and I am no longer
worthy of being called your son." (Luke 15:21, NLT)

Look at what the Father says . . .

"But his father said to the servants, 'Quick! Bring the finest
robe in the house and put it on him. Get a ring for his finger and
sandals for his feet.' " (Luke 15:22 NLT)

Don't delay. Why? So the father can get him restored before
the village wants to pass judgment. Nobody will see him in
his rags again. There is no waiting period for restoration.

Who had the finest robe in the family?
The paterfamilias—the father.

And the father's best robe would be saved for special
occasions. It would be what the older son would wear on his
wedding day. That was to be the greatest event of the family.
And look at who is wearing the father's best robe.

The ring had the family crest, it was the authentication and
authority to conduct family business. It goes even further.
What the father is doing is actually laying claim to all that
potentially belongs to the older son and says you're back in
the family.

"And kill the calf we have been fattening. We must celebrate with
a feast, for this son of mine was dead and has now returned to life.
He was lost, but now he is found. So the party began."
(Luke 15:23-24 NLT)

It wasn't every day that they had meat in their culture. It had to be for a special meal. And the most expensive meat would be the fatten calf. This is steak!

They had most likely had a ceremony when the son had left, a type of funeral for the son who had gone. That's why we see this reference to the father referring to his son as dead. This is how God loves you.

A DIVIDED FAMILY
The older brother was angry and wouldn't go in. (His father came out and begged him.)

"All these years I've slaved for you and never once refused to do a single thing you told me to. And in all that time you never gave me even one young goat for a feast with my friends."
(Luke 15:29 NLT)

If you do the right things with the wrong heart, it doesn't count . . . not to God.

Ironically, in this culture, it was the privilege of the oldest brother to be the host of the family parties. This was his party to throw! And he missed it.

The father's response was, "Dear son, you have always stayed by me, and everything I have is yours. We had to celebrate this happy day. For your brother was dead and has come back to life! He was lost, but now he is found!"

Jesus doesn't finish the story.
Why? Because he's genius!

It appears Jesus wants to give the religious leaders a chance to finish the story with a change of heart.

I think Jesus wants us to finish the story, too.

How are you going to finish the story?
How outrageous is your love?

Can you imagine . . . it clicks for the older brother, he goes inside, runs to his brother, hugs him and says, "Welcome home. I missed you." And the father smiles. There is joy!

Here's the missing piece to understanding the story. If you get this, you will get the story. It will change you forever.

Who is the party really celebrating . . . the wasteful son or the outrageous father? The party is celebrating the grace of the father. The hero of the story is not the prodigal or the older brother. The hero of the story is God. Do you have any idea how much God loves you?

BROKEN FAMILIES

I was on my way to Eastern Washington to speak at a church—my neighbor called, frantic, screaming and crying.

"Wes. She's dead. Can you get here?"

I called Kari. She immediately went to the house (she was the third person there on-site), and sure enough our 14-year-old neighbor was dead. She was a member of our church and youth group, watched our dog when we were gone. We traded pranks—she and her sisters chalked my driveway with a 49ers logo. And now she was gone.

To complicate the issue, this is a blended family. Lots of brokenness. Hard alcohol was involved. The 14-year-old has zero history with any of this, but the 16-year-old who had recently moved into the house with her dad/stepmom had a history of substance abuse.

We offered to take the 16-year-old into our house for a few days as we worked with this family to grieve and to forgive.

The 16-year-old, so broken—her downward spiral began the summer after her parents' divorce. It's not an excuse, simply a reality.

Our circle of friends-neighbors-community group came around this family (the parents came to the church— not the community group—the girls had both recently started coming).

We sat with the family.
Went to the funeral home together.
Brought meals every day.
Prayed together.
And cared for the 16-year-old (as the other siblings, step and blood relatives arrived).

On the third day, we began to prepare the family for the 16-year-old to return home. I talked with her dad. I told him she must hear these words: I love you no matter what. He said he was ready to do that. I talked with her stepmom, saying the words the Holy Spirit will help you say are, "I forgive you in Jesus' name" (I always add Jesus' name . . . because forgiveness almost always requires more grace than we possess). I prepared the 16-year-old to immediately hug both her parents and say, "I am so sorry. Will you forgive me?"

That evening, my neighbor's truck pulled up in front of my house. But only one car door opened. It was just dad. Sadly and slowly, he got out of the truck and began to walk up my driveway. Suddenly his phone rang and he yelled out, "Pastor, give me a moment. I'll be back."

The truck left.
The 16-year-old said, "I knew it. She will never forgive me."
Two minutes later
His truck returned

This time two doors opened
This time it was both dad and stepmom together,
walking up the hill

"What do I do? What do I do?" The 16-year-old whispers to
me. "You know what to do," I said.

The 16-year-old gets up and begins to walk to her parents.
Closer. Closer. And then suddenly they embrace.
Lots of tears
I am so sorry
Forgive me
I love you no matter what
I forgive you in Jesus' name

For five minutes I got to see what the Prodigal Son story
looks like in my driveway.
Five minutes!

Eventually the tears subside.
Voices quiet.
There is a lull.

Then the stepmom says to the 16-year-old, "Go get your
stuff, you're coming home."

What makes God's love outrageous? Two things. God says:
1. I love you no matter what.
2. I forgive you in Jesus' name.

Heaven is the family reunion you actually want to go to
because heaven is the family you have always wanted. The
Kingdom of Heaven burst into this world through Jesus and
he wants to teach us how to be a real family.

A while back, I was getting on Austin and probably for good
reasons. Right. We always have good reasons. Finally, he

said, "Can you say one nice thing about me today?"

I had developed the bad habit of always pointing out what he was doing wrong or could do better. It's not that we can't speak the truth in love. But that only works when there is an atmosphere of encouragement.

Do you build up your family or tear it down?

This is the family challenge.
Love the family you have . . . no matter what.
Practice encouraging your family members every day and see what God does in your family.

CHALLENGE #10
FAMILY

What I like about my family is . . .

_____

_____

_____

_____

_____

_____

_____

_____

TALK ABOUT IT

GROUP QUESTIONS

1. God IS a family. In the Bible family extended beyond blood. Who are the people closest to you that you consider family (oikos)? How have they helped you understand the Love of God?

2. God loves you enough to let you hit bottom. How has this truth played out in your own life? Where did God let you fall to before you turned your heart back to him? How has your life changed now in light of that tough love?

3. What makes God's love Outrageous? He says, "I love you no matter what, and I forgive you in Jesus name." In what ways has your view of God changed as you have experienced God the Father's forgiveness and outrageous love?

214

CHALLENGE #11
SABBATH

**REST ONE DAY,
SO YOU CAN ENJOY THE OTHER SIX**

And God blessed the
seventh day and
declared it holy,
because it was the
day when he rested from
all his work of creation.

GENESIS 2:3 NLT

Come to me, all of you
who are weary and carry heaven
burdens, and I
will give you rest.

JESUS
MATTHEW 11:28 NLT

CHALLENGE #11
SABBATH

How is your soul?
How do you sleep at night?

Apparently, trouble sleeping is actually a health problem.
More than 30 million Americans have this problem.

Sleep In America studies have linked sleep deficits with poor
performance, driving accidents, relationship problems,
mood problems, and depression.

Many people are too tired to realize how sleep deprived they
are, experts say. But they have slower reaction time, weaker
memory, and other thinking impairments.

Several major disasters have been linked, in part, with
too little sleep in the workplace, like Chernobyl and the
Exxon Valdez.

We just aren't getting enough sleep.
Adults need eight hours sleep.
Teens need nine.
And we're not getting it.

I read in a poll once that about one-third of all drivers
reported they had driven drowsy at least once per month
during the past year. That's downright frightening.

Everyone is sleepy and we don't know what to do about it.
Is there an app for that? Yes. There is.

SLEEP APP
I was having a little trouble sleeping last year.
. . . my daughter, Kali, suggested that I try the Sleep

Cycle App.

It measures your sleep.
You simply download the app, set your wake up time, and
set your iPhone face down on your bed. It records your
sleep. I don't know all the science behind it. But hey, it
was free.

It was free, but it didn't help.
At least not for me.
I kept getting low sleep scores, which was stressing me out.
The stress made it hard to sleep.
Plus, my daughter kept rubbing in my face her excellent
sleep scores.
I couldn't take the beating any longer.

So I switched.
I downloaded another app.
Sleep stories.
I love listening to someone read.
It puts me right to sleep.

When Kari and I were first married, she found out I had
never read all *The Chronicles of Narnia* series. I had no idea
that was a sin in the family she grew up in. So she started
reading me the Narnia stories. They were terrific. I fell fast
asleep. Usually she didn't know until the next day when I
had no idea what she was reading about.

Who's this Reepicheep? I asked.

Actually . . . I shouldn't have asked. Because she had been
reading about him for a few days. And that was the end
of that.

Now all I had was my sleep stories app.
That and . . . the rest that can only come from God.

Did you know God wants to help you sleep?

"In peace I will both lie down and sleep; for you alone, O Lord, make me dwell in safety." (Psalm 4:8, ESV)

God wants to help you rest.
One of God's primary strategies to help you rest each night is to teach you to rest one day a week. It's called the Sabbath.

"Remember to observe the Sabbath day by keeping it holy." (Exodus 20:8, NLT)

Before murder, before adultery, before stealing, before honoring mom and dad . . . Sabbath. Why? Sabbath is a day of rest.

Our culture thinks rest is a day off, a time for sleep or vacation. But have you ever come back from vacation and you are still tired? Or your day off feels like more of a work day than your work week.

What's rest?

God thinks rest is not just your body but your soul.
And not just with him but with each other.

Real rest refuels your body, your soul, and your relationships.

That's what Sabbath is for. It's holy.
And when you break the Sabbath, you break yourself.
You need a Sabbath.

Just look at the signs.

SIGNS YOU NEED A SABBATH

1. You start to look like your passport photo.

220

2. Paper or plastic is too big of a decision.
3. Last week you fell asleep—but you were standing up.
4. Your snooze button has a snooze button.
5. You think downtime is blinking.
6. Everything irritates you. Everything. This is irritating you.
7. You want to get away so bad, you plotted your own kidnapping.
8. The word exercise makes you sweat.
9. You've gone from decaf to espresso to a caffeine patch.
10. When you look at the clock, you aren't sure if it's a.m. or p.m.
11. You spend part of the day staring at squirrels in the lawn. And there are no squirrels . . . or a lawn.
12. You sleep with your laptop.

THE SABBATH DAY

In Genesis 1 and 2, we are introduced to the creation story. God spent six days working, creating, bringing order out of chaos.

Then.
Day 7.
Sabbath.

So the creation of the heavens and the earth and everything in them was completed. On the seventh day God had finished his work of creation, so he rested from all his work. And God blessed the seventh day and declared it holy, because it was the day when he rested from all his work of creation. (Genesis 2:1-3, NLT)

Day 7.
God rests.

Why did God rest?
Did he have to rest?

Three words jump off the pages at me.
1. Rested. 2. Blessed. 3. Holy.

God rested. The word for rest is the word "shabat" (it's where we get the word Sabbath). It means to cease, to stop, to complete. It can also be translated to celebrate. There God is, celebrating the work of his hands.

God works for six days and on the seventh day he rested. What does it mean he rested?

Growing up, we had rest time.
Rest time was boring. As a kid, you hate rest time. Why? It means you do nothing.

Is Sabbath a day of "nothing"?

What if we are looking at it wrong? In creation, what if Sabbath was the main event. Like God was creating and working toward this moment where he stopped and celebrated. What if Sabbath is a celebration that points to eternity?

Then it says *He blessed it.* The word there is "barak".

Three things God "baraked":
1. Living creatures. 2. Humans. 3. A day.

Why is God blessing a day? God blessed people and God blessed time. Why?

In the same way living creatures and humans are made to procreate, the Sabbath creates joy, life, and satisfaction in your soul. It refuels you with energy, creativity, vision, strength, optimism, buoyancy, clarity, and hope. This type of rest is blessed and life giving.

Then he says it is HOLY. This is a big deal. Rabbis believe
in the principle of first mention. Which means the first time in
the Bible a word is used, that gives us a definition for the rest
of the book and story.

The first thing God calls holy. You ready . . . TIME! A day.
We live in a world where we make spaces holy.

> Islam has mecca.
> Hinduism has the Ganges river.
> Paganism has Stonehenge.
> Baseball has Fenway park and Wrigley field.
> Seattle has the Space Needle.
> Kitsap has Silver City Restaurant.

God doesn't make a place holy. He makes time holy.
Think about that.
Fascinating.

Before God ever called something holy ground, there were
holy moments.

I did a wedding ceremony recently for a newlife couple. My
favorite moment of a wedding is always the moment that the
bride and the father of the bride walk down the aisle.

Oh . . . that is a holy moment.

And I have a great view. I'm standing there, looking right
back at that door that swings open. And the bride begins
to walk toward her groom. He is going nuts inside. I know.
I remember. It's the only part of the ceremony I remember.
The door opened. There was Kari and her dad. She started
walked toward me. I was like . . . (Baby you're a firework).

You know what's going to get me? That day—God willing—
that I walk a daughter down the aisle. I will be a complete
mess. Excited for her future. Ready to give her hand in

marriage. But . . . I will be walking S – L – O – W – L – Y.
They may have to play the song two times.

Because that moment will live in my heart for eternity.
There are moments that are holy.
They are special.

You can always make more money but you can't
make more time.
Wealth and kingdoms come and go.
But moments are here and then gone.
You can own space.
But God owns time.
It's his realm. And his kingdom is forever.
You can't own time but you can share it.
God shares time. He gives us the gift of Sabbath.

NO SABBATH
The story of the people of God goes through Genesis into
Exodus. Genesis ends with Joseph being second in command
in Egypt and bringing his entire family, "Israel," to Egypt.
Then a Pharaoh rose up who did not know Joseph and he
turned the family of God into slaves.

Slaves of production.
Pyramid builders.

God raises up Moses to lead the people out.
"Exodus" literally means a way out.
A way out of slavery.

Pharaoh won't budge. In Exodus 5 Pharaoh says, "Why are
you taking people away from their labor?
Get back to work!"
You are stopping them from working.
Make the work harder.
I will give you no more straw, but your work

will not be reduced.
Complete the work required of you.
Lazy, that's what you are. Lazy!

Pharaoh is relentless.
Make bricks. Make more bricks.
This is the voice of the Pharaoh in the back of our heads
screaming, "Work harder, work faster, work longer. Produce,
produce, produce. You're only as good as your daily quota.
Your worth comes from your production.
Make more bricks!"

Seven days. Seven days of making bricks.
There is no rhythm. There is no rest.

MAKING MUSIC
In music, there are rests. Quarter rest. Half rest. Full rest.
To have rhythm, there has to be breaks.
Music is not just the notes you play but the moments you
rest. Without rests, music descends into noise.

Is your life noise or are you making music?

Seven. Seven. Seven. Make bricks.
And then God comes in and says no.
You need rhythm.
You need rest.
Six and one. Six and one. Six and one.
This is the life of the child of God. Six and one.

Sabbath is about leaving Egypt behind.
It's about freedom.
It's the freedom from the sevens of making bricks.
It is the emancipation from Pharaoh's harsh rule.
It's gospel.

You are not a slave.

You are not a slave to production.
You are not a slave to consuming.
You are not a slave to selfies or busyness.
You were made to worship God and to enjoy his creation.

Sabbath is a way to say I have enough for today.
Tomorrow, I will return to work.
But today, it's Sabbath.
It's Sabbath. Get off the treadmill.

But the Pharaoh says no. No breaks. No three day holidays
to worship. No Sabbaths. No rests. No summer camp or
family vacation.

So God sends plagues to turn Pharaoh's heart. Finally,
Pharaoh lets them go . . . sort of. He lets them go and then
changes his mind. He sends the armies of Egypt after the
children of Israel. The people of God are trapped at the Red
Sea until . . . a miracle. The Red Sea parts and the people of
God are rescued.

They journey and find themselves at Mt. Sinai. It is here that
Moses travels to the top of the mountain to receive the 10
Commandments.

The first three commandments are about God.
1. You shall have no other gods before me. (Have one God).
2. You shall not make an idol in the form of anything.
    (Nothing comes before God.)
3. You shall not misuse the name of the Lord your God.
    (God's name is holy.)

The last six are about people.
4. Honor your father and your mother.
5. You shall not murder.
6. You shall not steal.

7. You shall not commit adultery (adultery = sex outside of marriage).
8. You shall not give false testimony (don't lie).
9. You shall not covet (covet = wants something that
1. belongs to someone else).

What is number four? Sabbath.

Remember to observe the Sabbath day by keeping it holy. You have six days each week for your ordinary work, but the seventh day is a Sabbath day of rest dedicated to the Lord your God. On that day, no one in your household may do any work. This includes you, your sons and daughters, your male and female servants, your livestock, and any foreigners living among you. For in six days the Lord made the heavens, the earth, the sea, and everything in them; but on the seventh day he rested. That is why the Lord blessed the Sabbath day and set it apart as holy. (Exodus 20:8-11, NLT)

Remember. Remember Genesis 1-2. Remember the garden.

Remember where we came from.

One theologian argues that the fourth commandment is a bridge between the first three and the last six. It is on the Sabbath that we connect our love for God with our love for people.

Later on in Deuteronomy 5, Moses recalls the Ten Commandments and puts a new twist on it. He doesn't say remember the garden. He says remember the exodus. **Remember you were once slaves to Egypt.** Moses knew the promised land was full of prosperity . . . and it is so easy to forget where you came from when all you experience is abundance. That is how Pharaoh became Pharaoh. Sabbath is a weekly exodus from the tyranny of production. You're free.

Then comes Jesus. Did you know Jesus spent most of his time healing on the Sabbath? You're like, time out. Does that count as work? Is he resting? Does Jesus Sabbath? That's what the religious leaders were wondering/accusing Jesus of. Jesus—you rebel—you work on the Sabbath!

So why does Jesus do this on the Sabbath?
Because Jesus understood that Sabbath has always been about healing.

Then Jesus said to them:
"The Sabbath was made to meet the needs of people, and not people to meet the requirements of the Sabbath. So the Son of Man is Lord, even over the Sabbath!" (Mark 2:27-28, NLT)

Sabbath is rest.
Sabbath is healing.
Sabbath is a message to our culture—God is going to heal this world and make all things new.

Life beats you up.
Jesus heals on the Sabbath.
Sabbath is a sign of God's love.
Sabbath is a game changer. One day of rest makes the other six days better.
How is Sabbath a game changer for your whole week? Let's get super practical.

SABBATH FREES YOU FROM BEING A SLAVE TO WORK

Let me remind you of this—work is a blessing.
The first thing God gave Adam was a job. Work is a gift.
Over-work is a curse.

Our culture never stops working and it is destroying our marriages and our families and our churches.

The people of Israel must keep the Sabbath day by observing it from generation to generation. This is a covenant obligation for all time. (Exodus 31:16 NLT)

Work is a gift from God, but God gives limits to his gifts so they don't enslave us. God gave us chocolate cake and it's a good thing, but if you eat the whole cake, it might kill you. It's the same thing with work.

There is a relationship that we are to have with work that is healthy, appropriate. The scriptures say, "If you don't work, you shouldn't eat." If we never work—that's a problem, and if we are always working—it's a problem, as well.

Sabbath brings freedom to our temptation to overwork.
What do you do on Sabbath?

One of the things you do is remember.
Remember what?
I was once a slave to sin. And now I am free.

In the book *The Sabbath*, Abraham Joshue Heschel writes, *"In every age, man must see himself as if he himself went out of Egypt."* Sabbath is a weekly exodus.

Also, Sabbath confronts our hidden fears about rest.
Fears about rest? What are you talking about?
The fear that if I rest and give one day to God
I won't have enough.
Have you ever felt guilty for taking a day off?
Have you ever laid in bed unable to sleep with anxiety about your work?

Sabbath confronts our deepest need: **You are valuable apart from what you produce.** You matter beyond your work. You matter because you are created by God.

SABBATH GIVES YOU
QUALITY TIME WITH GOD

Have you read the book The 5 Love Languages?

The premise is this: we each give and receive love differently.
To fully understand someone and grow your relationship
with them, you have to understand the way they feel most
loved and the way they show love naturally.

The Five Love Languages are:
1.   Words of Affirmation
2.   Acts of Service
3.   Receiving Gifts
4.   Quality Time
5.   Physical Touch

So I took the quiz. No surprise my top two were words of
affirmation and physical touch. I already knew that. Kari
already knew that. And I already know Kari's top two:
quality time and acts of service. Hmm. Can you see the
problem?

She wants me to do the dishes – I want her to tell me I'm
awesome. The more specific the better.

She wants to be together, undistracted.
I'm like, I would be a lot less distracted if you were rubbing
my back, or legs, or feet, really anything.

Quality time. That was really low on my list.
But it's really high on Kari's list.
And it's really high on God's list.
Here's the thing. I need it to be high on their list because
(and don't tell Kari) I need it, too. My marriage needs it. And
my soul needs it.

God loves quality time with you.

And he knows you need it and he knows just how to restore your soul.

God loves Sabbath.

He stopped. God made space to spend quality time with us. Think about that. God created space to be with you.

So . . . what are you doing with that?

This is a holy moment. God is creating quality time.

Here is what Kari thinks quality time looks like: slowing down, going somewhere else, making eye contact. Opening up about what's on your mind, talking about what's weighing you down. Listening. It's sharing time.

Is your marriage struggling?

Sabbath—quality time.

Is your relationship with your kids exhausting?

Sabbath—quality time.

Maybe you have a friendship and it just seems like distance is getting greater and greater?

Sabbath—quality time.

Sabbath is a gift from God. So are our relationships.

When you start to live Sabbath, it will become your family's favorite day of the week, and you will start to see more clearly how God is working in your relationships and in your spirit.

SABBATH RECHARGES YOUR SPIRITUAL BATTERIES

Right now, my cell phone is having a tougher time keeping a charge. It's like the battery takes really long to charge and runs out really fast. Does that describe you?

Are you someone who keeps your phone mostly charged—

most of the time? Or do you run it down to 0 percent?
I'm always in danger of 0 percent, and then kill the screen.
I don't want to over-exaggerate (cause, come on, that's not
me) but doesn't it feel like your life would end if your
phone died?

It holds everything you need: your contacts, your emails,
your memories, your money, your social identity. You can't
risk losing access to basically your life.

Think about it. What would you do? You might have to talk
to someone.

So I don't want my phone to die. But I'm always almost at
0 percent. So, I was given a portable phone charger—you
know what I'm talking about.

You can charge your phone without being near an outlet.
It's really nice because think of all the times you can't find
an outlet.

Okay, well, that's becoming less because we have outlets
everywhere now. Under your seat at Starbucks, there's a
power port; on an airplane, it's in front of you. But that's not
the point. The point is that we have to keep my phone alive.

So I was given a portable phone charger—little guy—plug it
in and my phone gets oxygen again. But here's the problem.
That little, portable phone charger kept dying.

So I got a new one—way better. It can charge your phone
four times faster and its battery life lasts longer, too. Except
. . . I'm not sure where the cord is. I can't find that cord. I've
got way too many cords.

Maybe I need a rest.
A phone Sabbath.

My phone needs a Sabbath.
My phone is like: you're Pharaoh. You're killing me. Make bricks, make bricks, make bricks! I'm just an iPhone 6; give me a break!

Your soul needs to recharge.
You need to go from red to green.
And it's not about figuring out how to get more done (portable chargers and more cords). Your soul needs a Sabbath.

And just like a dead phone is useless, so are you.

Here is the good news. God himself is the only source of power that can recharge your life. And he has given us the minimum time it should take to fill us back up. He said take a DAY . . . one day . . . take 24 hours of your week and RECHARGE.

We all need a Sabbath, a time to deliberately pause in order for us to rest and reconnect. We all need to recharge personally. We all need to reconnect, to plug in relationally with God, the only source of power.

When we take the time to Sabbath with God, he is able to recharge us. And when we are recharged, we are able to receive EVERYTHING he has for us. The Sabbath recharges us and it heals us.

This is the Sabbath challenge: Take one day this week and rest—ask God want he wants to do. Refuel your soul. Strengthen your relationships. Enjoy life. And rest.

Jesus wants to give you rest.

"Then Jesus said, "Come to me, all of you who are weary and carry heavy burdens, and I will give you rest." (Matthew 11:28 NLT)

Are you carrying a heavy burden?
Take the Sabbath challenge.
You'll sleep better.

CHALLENGE #11
SABBATH

My Sabbath day is: _____

What I do to recharge:

☐ _____

☐ _____

☐ _____

☐ _____

TALK ABOUT IT

GROUP QUESTIONS

1. Why is it so hard to Sabbath in our culture? Why is Sabbath so important for followers of Jesus?

2. How is your soul? (1- not good, 10- never better) Why?

3. What would you do if you had a whole day off to rest? What are some activities that feed your soul that you want to do this week?

CHALLENGE #12
ONE CRAZY
IDEA
DO WHAT GOD MADE YOU TO DO

Now faith is the
assurance of things
hoped for, the conviction
of things not seen.

HEBREWS 11:1 ESV

Having faith often
means doing what
others see
as crazy.

FRANCIS CHAN

CHALLENGE #12
ONE CRAZY IDEA

Have you ever felt like you were made for something more?
What do you think that is?
How do you find out?

If you want to know what you were made to do, you have to
talk to the one who made you. That's God.

God made you.
God made you to make a difference.
You may not know what it is, but God does. And God wants
to tell you what is. But just be ready . . . it might sound like a
crazy idea.

Crazy ideas. Those are the things God calls you to do that
require faith. I say faith because it's not something you can
do by yourself. You're going to need God, and you're going
to need God's people.

I believe that you are going to have a moment . . .

That moment when an idea hits you . . .
And . . .
You're excited. It's clear. It's crystal clear!

You know exactly what you're supposed to do.
There's passion.
There's vision.
There's a dream.

And then . . . there is doubt and fear.

That's not just an idea. That's a crazy idea!
It's never been done before.

It hasn't been done that way.
    I'm not ready.
        What if I fail?
            What will happen if I actually succeed?

There is only one way to find out.

This is you.
Moving beyond your fears and doubts.
Following Jesus.
Fueled by the Spirit.
Surrounded by the Church.
Listening. Hearing. Obeying.
And a whole lot of people experiencing the love of God
because you had . . . one crazy idea.

The Bible is filled with crazy ideas!

The tower of Babel.
Noah and the ark!
Abraham becomes a father.
Moses' Mom putting him in a basket.
Moses coming back.
Moses and the parting of the Red Sea!
Joshua and Jericho.
Gideon and 300 men defeat an army of 125,000 men.
Samson pushes down the walls of the pagan temple.
David and Goliath.
Shadrach, Meshach, and Abednego and the fiery furnace.
Daniel and the Lion's Den.
Jonah and the great fish.
Jesus and the cross.
Peter and Cornelius.

Paul and the missionary journeys.
. . . the whole book of Revelation!
All of them . . . crazy ideas.

And every crazy idea has one thing in common . . . faith.
Confidence in God.

How much confidence do you have in God?

Confidence that God is who he says he is and he can do
what he says he can do.

*Faith is the confidence that what we hope for will actually
happen; it gives us assurance about things we cannot see.
(Hebrews 11:1, NLT)*

It's easy to have confidence in God doing a crazy idea
through someone else, but what if God wants to do a crazy
idea through you?

Didn't Jesus say his disciples would do even greater things?
What do you think God wants to do through your life?
And where do you start? For Nehemiah, it was the broken
walls of Jerusalem.

The walls of Jerusalem are broken, symbolic of the nation of
Israel and the people of God. They are broken and everyone
just got used to them. We get used to things being broken.
And we lose our passion to do something about it. It's been
more than 100 years.

Rebuilding the broken walls of Jerusalem, that was
Nehemiah's crazy idea. Your crazy idea probably has to do
with rebuilding something that is broken, too.
The vision starts in one person's heart, Nehemiah. And God
works through Nehemiah to lead the people in rebuilding
the walls of Jerusalem in 52 days!

52 days! Broken more than 100 years. Rebuilt in 52 days.
What miracle could God do in your life, in our community,
if everyone worked together for 52 days? How did this

happen?

It started with Nehemiah serving as the cupbearer to the
King. The king is Artaxerxes.
He is the King of Persia.
It's 445 B.C.

See, 141 years earlier, the Babylonians put a fork in the
destruction of Jerusalem after a 20-year seize. The temple
burned, the walls destroyed, the young leaders deported
to Babylon in three waves over the 20-year period, and the
people decimated and scattered throughout the nations.

This is the exile.
You are forced to go and live somewhere else.
And your nation and family are gone.

This is one of the major events of the Old Testament.
The exodus—God's people being led by Moses out of
slavery in Egypt, and the exile—God's people being
scattered among the nations.

Babylon demolishes Jerusalem.
And 47 years later, they are conquered by the Medes
and the Persians.
The Persians rule the world during the books of Chronicles,
Ezra, Nehemiah, and Esther.

Nehemiah is busy in Susa protecting the King from
being poisoned. One of his brothers, Hanani, comes to visit
Nehemiah with bad news about the Jews who had returned
from captivity to rebuild Jerusalem.

It's a sad sight.
People are living in ruins.
They have homes. But the city has gone from being a place
of honor to an absolute dive. It's Ground Zero in Jerusalem.

They said to me, "Things are not going well for those who returned
to the province of Judah. They are in great trouble and disgrace.
The wall of Jerusalem has been torn down, and the gates have been
destroyed by fire." (Nehemiah 1:3, NLT)

It has been 141 years that the walls of Jerusalem (the pride
and protection of the city of God) have been broken, the
gates had been burned, and people have just kind of got
used to it. And this breaks Nehemiah's heart.

What breaks your heart?
Your crazy idea probably starts there.

THIS IS BROKEN!
Several years ago, I went to Washington DC for a kids
advocacy conference. This was an opportunity to find out
how to be a voice for children in poverty around the world.

Somehow we ended up on a red eye flight from Sea-Tac,
which I really don't enjoy. So, I had the idea to spend the
night at a nearby hotel, park, and fly.

Wanting to be a good steward of our resources I found the
best deal on a super cheap hotel. It wasn't until we drove up
to it that I discovered why. It was the cheapest hotel because
of its location. The stores in the neighborhood had bars on
the windows and next door to the hotel was a not-so-nice
establishment named the Déjà Vu.

Sketchy.
Let's just say, I slept in my jeans.

We fell asleep to my audio Bible app, but it would be short.
The room next door woke us up.
On the hour.
One-two-three times.
Each time someone closed a door, walked down the steps,

got into a car, and left. And someone stayed behind.

Broken.
Our world is broken.
The walls to our city, our community, our nation, our world
are broken.

On the trip, I met a pastor. Their church is surrounded by
strip joints and the women of their church go inside and give
gifts to the women who work there. They say, "We love you.
If you ever want to talk let us know."

To date, 42 women have left that industry and one of the key
volunteers of the church is an ex-stripper.

That night, God said, "Wes, Brandon—don't get used to
what's broken. Don't get used to broken walls. Let the
brokenness break your heart."
That's what happened to Nehemiah.

When I heard this, I sat down and wept. In fact, for days I
mourned, fasted, and prayed to the God of heaven.
(Nehemiah 1:4, NLT)

Nehemiah mourned, fasted, and prayed.
Don't skip this step.

God wants to show you what he sees every day.

And break your heart with the things that break his heart.
Instead of judging people—weep with them.

Do you know someone going through a broken marriage?
Weep with them.

Someone who has come forward to get help with an
addiction?

Weep with them.

Someone who feels abandoned and totally alone?
Weep with them.

Before you are tempted to jump in and rebuild—mourn,
fast, pray. Let it break your heart. Then, admit you're part of
the problem. To be part of the solution, you have to include
yourself in the problem.

Own the problem.
Own the solution.
This is what Nehemiah does.

*Then I said, "O Lord, God of heaven, the great and awesome God
who keeps his covenant of unfailing love with those who love him
and obey his commands, listen to my prayer! Look down and see
me praying night and day for your people Israel. I confess that we
have sinned against you. Yes, even my own family
and I have sinned!" (Nehemiah 1:5-6, NLT)*

It isn't enough to point out the brokenness in the world.
Start with the brokenness in your own life. It will give you
the humility needed to lead.

We are all broken.
So confess your sin.

Does the church do that?
Do I do that?

When I see brokenness—is that my response?
No. I'm more like, I confess that you have sinned. You've
really screwed up your life. Now back off as I come in and
fix it for you.

This approach never works for me.

Why? I am not the Messiah. And neither are you.
We can't fix the deep brokenness in the world.
We can point to Jesus.
And we can get involved. Amazing things happen when we
get everyone involved.

Nehemiah starts by getting King Artaxerxes involved.
He asks the King for paid leave, materials, and safe travel.
. . . and he gets it.

It's amazing the favor you get when you serve well.

Who has God asked you to serve?
You may not realize it, but perhaps you are perfectly
positioned to do something about the brokenness
that you see.

Nehemiah gets what he needs to get started and heads off
800 miles to see the brokenness firsthand. Go and see the
broken walls.

I got the opportunity to go and see the power of child
sponsorship in Africa, and the difference it makes when I
send $40 a month to help a child in poverty.

I'd seen commercials.

Heard stories.
Talked to people who had been there.

But nothing could replace walking down the street.
The smell of brokenness.
The sight of malnutrition.

I could see the visual difference between children who were
sponsored and those who weren't.

I will not need to see it again to know I need to do something
about it. I can't do everything. But I can sponsor one child.
Now our family sponsors four.

I can't sponsor every child.
But I can be a voice.
What if everyone sponsored one child in poverty?
What if you skipped one lunch a week and used that money
to sponsor a child in poverty?

If Jesus could feed 5,000 people with one kid's meal, could
Jesus feed the world with our lunch?

You can't rebuild the broken walls by yourself, but your
crazy idea might be someone else's crazy idea, too. Turned
out there was a lot of people who wanted to rebuild the
walls of Jerusalem.

A great vision attracts a lot of people.
Who do you need to talk to?
Who needs to get involved?

Nehemiah travels 800 miles to see the brokenness.
People gather around him.
He has backing, he has resources, and he has a dream.

*"You know very well what trouble we are in. Jerusalem lies in
ruins, and its gates have been destroyed by fire. Let us rebuild the
wall of Jerusalem and end this disgrace!" (Nehemiah 2:17, NLT)*

This is a vision that even a child can understand.
Let's rebuild the walls.
It's clear.
It's passionate.
And people respond.

Everyone gets started.

But not everyone is excited.

There will be opposition. For Nehemiah it was people like Sanballat, Tobiah, and Geshem the Arab.

Nehemiah faced opposition and so will you.
Expect it.

Opposition is good.
It's why God allows it. So don't quit.
Opposition can make you stronger, purify your motives, improve your plans, and bring a group of people together.

It isn't just the walls that need to be rebuilt, it's you.
It's your teammates. It's the church.

Nehemiah refuses to be discouraged or distracted.
Instead he stays focused.
He helps everyone find their place on the wall.

Where is your place on the wall?

For Eliashib, the high priest and the other priests, it was rebuilding the Sheep Gate. For the sons of Hassenaah, their place on the wall was the Fish Gate. For Joiada and Meshullam, it was the Old City Gate. For many people, their place on the wall was near their homes working with their families.

What if your place on the wall isn't somewhere distant, but close to where you live? What if rebuilding the broken walls also strengthens the relationships in your family?

Serving together brings families together.
Your crazy idea will not only bless your community, it will bless your family.

Nehemiah has everyone involved.
But his enemies are still trying to stop him.
Sanballat, Tobiah, and Geshem send him a message to go
to the plains of Ono and ask Nehemiah to meet them there.
Four times they send the same message.

Meet with us at once . . . I am engaged in a great work . . .
Meet with us at once . . . I am engaged in a great work . . .
Four times . . . and then a fifth time . . .

What does Nehemiah say?

"I am engaged in a great work, so I can't come." (Nehemiah 6:3, NLT)

Laser focus.
Bulldog determination.
No sideways energy.
That's what it takes to finish.
A lot of people start a crazy idea, but it takes tremendous
determination and focus to finish.

And in 52 days—with everyone working—the wall is
completed!

*So on October 2 the wall was finished—just fifty-two days after
we had begun. When our enemies and the surrounding nations
heard about it, they were frightened and humiliated. They realized
this work had been done with the help of our God. (Nehemiah
6:15-16 NLT)*

What could God do in your community in the next 52 days?
What is broken in your community or the world that God
wants you to rebuild?

This is the crazy idea challenge.
Be ready for God to show you a need.

Maybe the first one will look really small. Maybe it's just an opportunity to see if you will respond. But be ready for God to show you a broken wall.

Let it break your heart. Enough to get involved. See who else wants to get involved. Make a simple plan. Stay determined. Don't get distracted. And see what God does with your one crazy idea.

CHALLENGE #12
ONE CRAZY IDEA

My crazy idea is: _____

My plan is:

☐ _____

☐ _____

☐ _____

☐ _____

My people are:

☐ _____

☐ _____

☐ _____

TALK ABOUT IT

GROUP QUESTIONS

1. Every crazy idea has one thing in common, Faith. Think about a time you sensed God asking you to do something that was going to stretch your faith. How did you respond?

2. Crazy Ideas often start with a concern. Something breaks our heart and we know that something needs to change. What crazy idea has God placed in your heart?

3. What are some things in your life right now that could distract you from your crazy idea? How can you allow God to help you focus on what you are being called to do?

SECTION 3
STORIES

This is the fun part.

I can't wait to hear the stories of how God will use you to push back darkness; to forgive in Jesus' name; and to transform your neighborhood, your workplace and your family with the Freedom of the Gospel . . . As we each take the challenge to be:

PEOPLE BECOMING THE CHURCH

Start to collect your stories here AND
email them to me at wes.davis@newlife.tv:

_____

_____

_____

_____

_____

_____

_____

PEOPLE BECOMING
THE CHURCH PRAYER

Jesus, I am your disciple.
I want to show your love
to this world.

These are your hands.
These are your feet.
Give me your heart.
Speak through me.
Show me what you see.
Use me today.

For your glory.
Amen.

Made in the USA
Lexington, KY
27 December 2017